T0196056

Deep Calls to Deep

The discovery and the breaking of the billows and waves of good news

GIDEON AGYEMANG

WESTBOW
PRESS®
A DIVISION OF THOMAS NELSON
& ZONDERVAN

This book is a work of non-fiction. Unless otherwise noted, the author and the publisher make no explicit guarantees as to the accuracy of the information contained in this book and in some cases, names of people and places have been altered to protect their privacy.

WestBow Press books may be ordered through booksellers or by contacting:

WestBow Press
A Division of Thomas Nelson & Zondervan
1663 Liberty Drive
Bloomington, IN 47403
www.westbowpress.com
1 (866) 928-1240

ISBN: 978-1-9736-9026-9 (sc)
ISBN: 978-1-9736-9027-6 (e)

Print information available on the last page.

WestBow Press rev. date: 04/18/2020

DEDICATION

I dedicate this output to all of humanity especially the generations yet to be created. And also to the people of faith in Christ Jesus.

ACKNOWLEDGEMENT

I would like to acknowledge the incredible impact that family and friends have made in my life, for all their patience towards my complexity and most importantly these influencers:

- *William Wilberforce*
- *Martin Luther King Jnr.*
- *Myles Egbert Munroe*
- *Peter Derek Vaughan Prince*
- *John Charles Maxwell*
- *Mensa Anamoa Otabil*

PROLOGUE

***Deep Calls to Deep:** the search, the discovery and the
breaking of the billows and waves of good news.*

'Bright eyes encourage the heart; good news nourishes the body. Cold water to someone who is thirsty -- that's what good news from a distant land is.' [Proverbs 15:30, 25:25 ISV]

'Light in a messenger's eyes brings joy to the heart, and good news gives health to the bones. Like cold water to a weary soul is good news from a distant land.' [Proverbs 15:30, 25:25 NIV]

The world at large needs cold water as our souls are weary, we are thirsty for good news to nourish our body and health to our bones. But where can we get this cold water from? From where can we receive the good news? Only from a distant land, from a messenger who has light in the eyes, bright eyes in order to encourage and bring joy to our hearts for none from our world can serve us this cold water we all need. Humanity is like the deer that is panting for streams of water, our soul is thirsting for something that is living and refreshing.

The *five* main questions of the gospel;

- Where or Who is the gospel from? Source or Origin.
- What or Who is the gospel about? Center Focus.
- Who or What is the gospel for? Target.
- Why is it the gospel? Reason.
- What must be done with the gospel?

The gospel which is the good news has an origin, who is the good news coming from, where is this good news coming from? If it is good news, then it has a content, what is the content and focus of this good news? What good news is carried in it? Who are the audience for this good news, this news must be read to which people? What at all make this news good? Why is it good news?

- **G**od created mankind in His image and likeness to *be*; relate and rule with Him forever. *[Genesis 1:26 NIV]*
- **O**ne man's sin separated us from Him forever. *[Isaiah 59:2 NIV]*
- **S**in cannot be removed by the sinful man and the penalty of sin cannot be paid by the sinful man.
- **P**rice for the penalty of sin was paid only by the Righteous One, Jesus Christ the only Son of God. [1 Peter 3:18 NIV]
- **E**veryone is.
- **L**ost.

The gospel is **G**od's **O**ffering of **S**alvation **P**roclaimed to **E**veryone, everyone who believes in Him alone is saved to **E**xperience **E**verlasting **L**ife. It is about God's **g**overnment of the kingdom, His **o**ffering of love, His **s**alvation from sin and darkness, His **p**romise, plan, purpose, His **e**verlasting **l**ife. The gospel is God's redemptive plan and must be faithfully and fully acclaimed and confessed, it must be freely and firmly proclaimed and professed.

CHAPTER ONE

The Genesis: The First Man Adam.

All things have a beginning, a point in time of their inception. Just as every product has the producer, every book an author, every code the coder, so too man has a creator. The maker of man is the builder of all things; spiritual and physical, heavens and earth. Again, just as there is a reason for everything, so there is a reason for man being created and placed specifically on the earth.

The Beginning:

"In the beginning God created the heavens and the earth. Then God said, "Let us make mankind in our image, in our likeness, so that they may rule over the fish in the sea and the birds in the sky, over the livestock and all the wild animals, and over all the creatures that move along the ground." So, God created mankind in his own image, in the image of God he created them; male and female he created them. God blessed them and said to them, "Be fruitful and increase in number; fill the earth and subdue it. Rule over the fish in the sea and the birds in the sky and over every living creature that moves on the ground." Then God said, "I give you every seed-bearing plant on the face of the whole earth and every tree that has fruit with seed in it. They will be yours for food. And to all the beasts of the earth and all the birds in the sky and all the creatures that move along the ground—everything that has the breath of life in it—I give every green plant for food." And it was so. God saw all that he had made, and it was very good." [Genesis 1:1, 26-31 NIV]

The key ideas from the passage of scripture is that;

- *Heaven and earth had a beginning. In this beginning was the beginning of the heavens and the earth. [Genesis 1:1 NIV]*
- *Heaven and earth were created by God. [Genesis 1:1 NIV]*

- *Mankind was created by God in His image and likeness. Mankind has the unique essence of being in the image and likeness of the God of creation. [Genesis 1:27 NIV]*
- *Mankind was to rule over the other creations; fish, birds, livestock, wild animals, all moving creatures. [Genesis 1:28 NIV]*
- *Mankind was created male and female. [Genesis 1:27 NIV]*
- *Mankind was blessed by God to "be fruitful and increase in number, fill the earth, and subdue it". [Genesis 1:28 NIV] Man has the inherent capacity of seed to produce fruit in increasing number such that the seed fruit fills the earth and subdues it.*
- *Mankind was commanded to eat freely with the only exception being not to eat from the tree of knowledge of good and evil. [Genesis 2:17 NIV]*

"This is the account of the heavens and the earth when they were created, when the Lord God made the earth and the heavens. Now no shrub had yet appeared on the earth and no plant had yet sprung up, for the Lord God had not sent rain on the earth and there was no one to work the ground, but streams came up from the earth and watered the whole surface of the ground. Then the Lord God formed a man from the dust of the ground and breathed into his nostrils the breath of life, and the man became a living being. Now the Lord God had planted a garden in the east, in Eden; and there he put the man he had formed. The Lord God made all kinds of trees grow out of the ground—trees that were pleasing to the eye and good for food. In the middle of the garden were the tree of life and the tree of the knowledge of good and evil. A river watering the garden flowed from Eden; from there it was separated into four headwaters. The name of the first is the Pishon; it winds through the entire land of Havilah, where there is gold. (The gold of that land is good; aromatic resin and onyx are also there.) The name of the second river is the Gihon; it winds through the entire land of Cush. The name of the third river is the Tigris; it runs along the east side of Ashur. And the fourth river is the Euphrates.

The Lord God took the man and put him in the Garden of Eden to work it and take care of it. And the Lord God commanded the man, "You are free to eat from any tree in the garden; but you must not eat from the tree of the knowledge of good and evil, for when you eat from it you will certainly die. The Lord God said, "It is not good for the man to be alone. I will make a helper suitable for him." Now the Lord God had formed out of the ground all the wild animals and all the birds in the sky. He brought them to the man to see what he would name them; and whatever the man called each living creature, that was its name. So, the man gave names to all the livestock, the birds in the sky and all the wild animals. But for Adam no suitable helper was found. So, the Lord God caused the man to fall into a deep sleep; and while he was sleeping, he took one of the man's ribs and then closed up the place with flesh. Then the Lord God made a woman from the rib he had taken out of the man, and he brought her to the man. The man said, "This is now bone of my bones and flesh of my flesh; she shall be called 'woman,' for she was taken out of man." That is why a man leaves his father and mother and is united to his wife, and they become one flesh. Adam and his wife were both naked, and they felt no shame."" [Genesis 2:4-25 NIV]

This passage of scripture also contains key ideas, some of which are:

- *The body of man was formed from the dust of the ground. [Genesis 2:7 NIV]*
- *God breathed into the body of man the breath of life. [Genesis 2:7 NIV]*
- *Man is a living being. [Genesis 2:7 NIV]*
- *Man was placed in a garden with resources on earth. [Genesis 2:8 NIV]*
- *Man was to work and care for the garden. [Genesis 2:15 NIV]*
- *Man was commanded as to what to eat and what not to eat and the consequences thereof. [Genesis 2:16-17 NIV]*
- *Man was alone, and to God it was not good. [Genesis 2:18 NIV]*
- *God made a helper suitable for him, took the "rib" of man to form a woman. [Genesis 2:18,21-22 NIV]*
- *God brought the woman to the man. [Genesis 2:22 NIV]*
- *Man said and called the helper suitable "woman" because she was taken from man. [Genesis 2:23 NIV]*

From all the above ideas, the male man was made first before the female man. God placed all things under the charge of all mankind with the male man as the head and the woman as the suitable helper. Every command of God was given to the male man first.

God placed His all in all into man. Someone recorded it same somewhere and said that; "*When I consider your heavens, the work of your fingers, the moon and the stars, which you have set in place, what is mankind that you are mindful of them, human beings that you care for them? You have made them a little lower than the divine [Yourself, God] and crowned them with glory and honor. You made them rulers over the works of your hands; you put everything under their feet: all flocks and herds, and the animals of the wild, the birds in the sky, and the fish in the sea, all that swim the paths of the seas.*" [Psalm 8:3-8 NIV]

The Loss:

"*Now the serpent was more crafty than any of the wild animals the Lord God had made. He said to the woman, "Did God really say, 'You must not eat from any tree in the garden'?" The woman said to the serpent, "We may eat fruit from the trees in the garden, but God did say, 'You must not eat fruit from the tree that is in the middle of the garden, and you must not touch it, or you will die.'" "You will not certainly die," the serpent said to the woman. "For God knows that when you eat from it your eyes will be opened, and you will be like God, knowing good and evil." When the woman saw that the fruit of the tree was good for food and pleasing to the eye, and also desirable for gaining wisdom, she took some and ate it. She also gave some to her husband, who was with her, and he ate it. Then the eyes of both of them were opened, and they realized they were naked; so, they sewed fig leaves together and made coverings for themselves. Then the man and his wife heard the sound of the Lord God as he was walking in the garden in the cool of the day, and they hid from the Lord God among the trees of the garden. But the Lord God called to the man, "Where are you?" He answered, "I heard you in the garden, and I was afraid because I was naked; so, I hid." And he said, "Who told you that you were naked? Have you eaten from the tree that I commanded you not to eat from?" The man said, "The woman you put here with me —she gave me some fruit from the tree, and I ate it." Then the Lord God said to the woman, "What is this you have done?" The woman said, "The serpent deceived me, and I ate." So, the Lord God said to the serpent, "Because you have done this, "Cursed are you above all livestock and all wild animals! You will crawl on your belly and you will eat dust all the days of your life. And I will put enmity between you and the woman, and between your offspring and hers; he will crush your head, and you will strike his heel." To the woman he said, "I will make your pains in childbearing very severe; with painful labor you will give birth to children. Your desire will be for your husband, and he will rule over you." To Adam he said, "Because you listened to your wife and ate fruit from the tree about which I commanded you, 'You must not eat from it,' "Cursed is the ground because of you; through painful toil you will eat food from it all the days of your life. It will produce thorns and thistles for you, and you will eat the plants of the field. By the sweat of your brow you will eat your food until you return to the ground, since from it you were taken; for dust you are and to dust you will return." Adam named his wife Eve, because she would become the mother of all the living. The Lord God made garments of skin for Adam and his wife and clothed them. And the Lord God said, "The man has now become like one of us, knowing good and evil. He must not be allowed to reach out his hand and take also from the tree of life and eat, and live forever." So, the Lord God banished him from the Garden of Eden to work the ground from which he had been taken. After he drove the man out, he placed on the east side of the Garden of Eden cherubim and a flaming sword flashing back and forth to guard the way to the tree of life." [Genesis 3:1-24 NIV]*

The passage of scripture reveals tremendous events and their consequences. The distortion in the garden of delight, the loss of perfect relationship and rulership between man and the Creator by an act of deception that led to disobedience.

- *The crafty serpent questioned the word of God to the woman. [Genesis 3:1 NIV]*
- *The crafty serpent misrepresented the word of God to the woman. [Genesis 3:4 NIV]*
- *The crafty serpent disproved the truthfulness of the word of God to the woman. [Genesis 3:4 NIV]*
- *The crafty serpent presented an alternative word to the woman. [Genesis 3:5 NIV]*
- *The woman misrepresented the word of God to the crafty serpent. [Genesis 3:3 NIV]*
- *The woman accepted the alternate word of the crafty serpent. [Genesis 3:6 NIV]*
- *The woman acted upon the word of the crafty serpent. [Genesis 3:6 NIV]*
- *The woman rejected the word of God. [Genesis 3:6 NIV]*
- *The man who was "with" the woman was silent. [Genesis 3:6 NIV]*

- *The man who was "with" the woman did not (re)present the word of God to the crafty serpent. [Genesis 3:6 NIV]*
- *The man who was "with" the woman did not disprove the alternate word of the crafty serpent. [Genesis 3:6 NIV]*
- *The man who was "with" the woman did not reject the alternate word of the crafty serpent. [Genesis 3:6 NIV]*
- *The man who was "with" the woman accepted the fruit and he ate it. [Genesis 3:6 NIV]*
- *The eyes of both of them were opened. [Genesis 3:7 NIV] The first effect of the act of disobedience was a shift to the 'senses', the eyes of mankind now were opened.*
- *They realized they were naked. [Genesis 3:7 NIV] The senses effect brought about a self-realization of "nakedness", a sense of being empty, the glorious covering of their maker was taken off.*
- *They sewed fig leaves together and made coverings for themselves. [Genesis 3:7 NIV] The next action of man was self-covering, trying to cover up and replace the glorious covering of the maker. An action from self to replace the action of the maker.*
- *They hid from the Lord God among the trees of the garden when they heard the sound of the Lord God as he was walking in the garden in the cool of the day. [Genesis 3:8 NIV] Again, man goes on to "hide", fear has now been generated in man's heart, after they realized their nakedness due to their actions of disobedience and upon hearing the voice of the maker they hid.*
- *The Lord God called to the man, "Where are you?" [Genesis 3:9 NIV] Man was now not found in his disposition and position; man has lost his place and the maker was looking to find them from where they are.*
- *The Lord God asked their disposition with respect to their position with Him; "Who told you that you were naked? Have you eaten from the tree that I commanded you not to eat from?" [Genesis 3:11 NIV]*
- *The man said, "The woman you put here with me —she gave me some fruit from the tree, and I ate it." [Genesis 3:12 NIV] Man shifts responsibility from himself to the woman and to God, the reason for his actions he relegates to the woman you God put here with me.*
- *The Lord God said to the woman, "What is this you have done?" The woman said, "The serpent deceived me, and I ate." [Genesis 3:13 NIV] The woman was no different from the man, she shifted the blame to the serpent.*
- *The Lord God reduced the serpent, from its original state to below all livestock and wild animals such that it began to have to crawl on its belly and eat dust all the days of its life. God thus placed an enmity between the serpent and the woman, between the offspring of both. The serpent was cursed among its kind, again enmity was placed between the "serpent" and "the woman" and between "the offspring of the woman" and that of the serpent. This enmity was the struggle that*

would result in the offering of the woman "crushing" the "head of the serpent" and that of the serpent "striking his heel". [Genesis 3:14-15 NIV]

- To the woman, the Lord, made her pains in child bearing very severe such that she gives birth to her children with painful labor whiles her desire became that of her husband, who would then rule over her. The curse of the woman was specific to her process of bringing life into the world because she was the man with the womb for life to be produced, instead of the process of being without pains now she was going to have pains and the pains was also going to be very severe. Again her "desire" will now be for her husband with the husband "ruling over" her. [Genesis 3:16 NIV]

- To Adam, the Lord, said to him of his disobedience against Him and for listening to his wife, thereby eating the fruit from the tree about which he was commanded not to it, the land for which he was to eat food from was now going to be done through painful toil all the days of his life. The ground was now going to be barren and unyielding, producing thorns and thistles such that Adam was to now eat the plants of the filed by the sweat of his brow until he returned to the ground, since from it he was taken in the physical body form. The curse of the man Adam was directed towards the creation he was to rule over, work and care for, the creation; "ground" was cursed, it was placed under bondage by its creator. Instead of it being fruitful and productive, now it was going to produce "thorns and thistles". Man was now going to have to toil painfully by the sweat of his brow to be able to eat food all the days of his life. And the ultimate effect of it all. Man will "certainly die"! Death was now an inevitability with man. [Genesis 3:17-19 NIV]

- Adam named his wife Eve, because she would become the mother of all the living. [Genesis 3:20 NIV]

- The Lord God made garments of skin for Adam and his wife and clothed them. And due to man's ability to now know good and evil, the Lord God did not allow him to reach out his hand and take also from the tree of life and eat, and live forever. So, the Lord God removed him from the Garden of Eden to work the ground from which he had been taken, this was to protect man from forever living in the state of sin and death from eating the fruit of life. Upon driving the man out, He placed on the east side of the Garden of Eden cherubim and a flaming sword flashing back and forth to guard the way to the tree of life. [Genesis 3:21-24 NIV]

The Principles -

- "Sin entered the world through one man, and death through sin, and in this way, death came to all people, because all sinned. Death reigned from the time of Adam; sin reigned in death. The wages of sin is death. Through the disobedience of the one man, many were made sinners; all have sinned and fall short of the glory of God." [Romans 5:12, 14 NIV]

- *The sin of the world is that one man disobeyed-sinned, so all men sinned; "All sinned and fall short of the glory of God." [Romans 3:23 NIV]*
- *The divine remedy is that the offspring of the woman will crush "the head" of the serpent and it will strike "his heel". [Genesis 3:15 NIV]*
- *Curse is to deprive of ability to produce or function as originally designed and intended; "The creation waits in eager expectation for the children of God to be revealed. For the creation was subjected to frustration, not by its own choice, but by the will of the one who subjected it, in hope that the creation itself will be liberated from its bondage to decay and brought into the freedom and glory of the children of God. We know that the whole creation has been groaning as in the pains of childbirth right up to the present time." [Romans 8:19-22 NIV]*

CHAPTER TWO

The Father of Many Nations, Abraham.

After the loss and fall of the first man on earth to the induction and seduction of the crafty serpent to disobey the law of their maker, mankind was now under a state and stage of reduction and deduction. All the ills of sin and the works of it continued until the time the maker of the heavens and earth made a divine decision to initiate His ultimate counsel to salvage mankind from the effects and consequences of disobedience. The maker of heaven and earth stepped into the earth and identified a man called Abram to facilitate His divine plan of rescue. This plan went through a series of events in sequence, from the moment of him being called, separated, and being given a divine covenant based on an oath from the greater one.

The Call and the Blessing:

"The Lord had said to Abram, "Go from your country, your people and your father's household to the land I will show you. I will, make of you a great nation; I will bless you and make your name great, so that you will be a blessing. I will bless them who bless you and curse him who curses you, and in you all families of the earth will be blessed."" *[Genesis 12:1-3 MEV]*

The Lord called Abram from his own country, people and father's household to make him into a great nation, making his name great so that he would be a blessing to all families of the earth. *[Genesis 12:1-3 NIV]*

The Separation and the Blessing:

"All the land that you see I will give to you and to your descendants forever. I will make your descendants like the dust of the earth, so that if a man could number the dust of the earth, then your

descendants could also be numbered. Arise, and walk throughout the land across its length and its width, for I will give it to you." [Genesis 13:15-17 MEV]

In the blessing of the Lord, Abram's descendants were to inherit the land forever, such that his descendants would be like the dust of the earth, out numbering the dust of the earth if a man was to number them. *[Genesis 13:15-16 MEV]*

The King -- Priest of Righteousness and Peace and the Blessing:

"Then Melchizedek king of Salem brought out bread and wine. He was the priest of God Most High. And he blessed him and said, "Blessed be Abram by God Most High, Creator of heaven and earth; and blessed be God Most High, who has delivered your enemies into your hand." Then Abram gave him a tenth of everything." [Genesis 14:18-20 MEV]

The Covenant -- Oath and the Blessing:

Time passed, seasons came and went away and it seemed that the promises made to Abram by the Lord were delaying, so the *word of the Lord* came to Abram in a *vision [Genesis 15:1 NIV]* to give assurance and insurance to Abram that the Lord would surely fulfill this promise to him. The *word of the Lord* became Abram's *shield* and *great reward. [Genesis 15:1 NIV]* The assurance and insurance of the Lord was based on a covenant, a covenant where the *greater* -- the Sovereign Lord -- makes a commitment to the *lesser* --Abram. The Sovereign Lord committed to fulfilling His promise to Abram such that in the covenant, if the greater was to break His word to the lesser, the life of the greater was to end, God's very existence was to cease if He failed to faithfully do what He was promising to Abram.

"After this, the word of the Lord came to Abram in a vision: "Do not be afraid, Abram. I am your shield, your very great reward." But Abram said, "Sovereign Lord, what can you give me since I remain childless and the one who will inherit my estate is Eliezer of Damascus?" And Abram said, "You have given me no children; so a servant in my household will be my heir." Then the word of the Lord came to him: "This man will not be your heir, but a son who is your own flesh and blood will be your heir." He took him outside and said, "Look up at the sky and count the stars —if indeed you can count them." Then he said to him, "So shall your offspring be."

Abram believed the Lord, and he credited it to him as righteousness. He also said to him, "I am the Lord, who brought you out of Ur of the Chaldeans to give you this land to take possession of it." But Abram said, "Sovereign Lord, how can I know that I will gain possession of it?" So, the Lord said to him, "Bring me a heifer, a goat and a ram, each three years old, along with a dove and a young pigeon." Abram brought all these to him, cut them in two and arranged the halves opposite each other; the birds, however, he did not cut in half. Then birds of prey came down on the carcasses, but Abram drove them away.

As the sun was setting, Abram fell into a deep sleep, and a thick and dreadful darkness came over him. Then the Lord said to him, "Know for certain that for four hundred years your descendants will be strangers in a country not their own and that they will be enslaved and mistreated there. But I will punish the nation they serve as slaves, and afterward they will come out with great possessions. You, however, will go to your ancestors in peace and be buried at a good old age. In the fourth generation your descendants will come back here, for the sin of the Amorites has not yet reached its full measure." When the sun had set and darkness had fallen, a smoking firepot with a blazing torch appeared and passed between the pieces. On that day the Lord made a covenant with Abram and said, "To your descendants I give this land, from the Wadi of Egypt to the great river, the Euphrates — the land of the Kenites, Kenizzites, Kadmonites, Hittites, Perizzites, Rephaites, Amorites, Canaanites, Girgashites and Jebusites."" [Genesis 15:1-21 NIV]

The Test and the Blessing:

Now God had made a sovereign promise to Abram [*many, multitude*] and changed his name thereafter to Abraham [*exalted father, father of many*]. [*Genesis 17:4-5 NIV*] But the Lord wanted to test the sincerity of the heart of Abraham towards Him, so He sets up a journey for Abraham to a place to offer a sacrifice to Him. Yet the problem of this sacrifice is that the very seed of promise in whom the Lord was to fulfill His covenant and who is the beloved of Abraham was to be the offering for the sacrifice.

"Sometime later God tested Abraham. He said to him, "Abraham!"

"Here I am," he replied. Then God said, "Take your son, your only son, whom you love—Isaac—and go to the region of Moriah. Sacrifice him there as a burnt offering on a mountain I will show you." Early the next morning Abraham got up and loaded his donkey. He took with him two of his servants and his son Isaac. When he had cut enough wood for the burnt offering, he set out for the place God had told him about. On the third day Abraham looked up and saw the place in the distance. He said to his servants, "Stay here with the donkey while I and the boy go over there. We will worship and then we will come back to you." Abraham took the wood for the burnt offering and placed it on his son Isaac, and he himself carried the fire and the knife. As the two of them went on together, Isaac spoke up and said to his father Abraham, "Father?" "Yes, my son?" Abraham replied.

"The fire and wood are here," Isaac said, "but where is the lamb for the burnt offering?" Abraham answered, "God himself will provide the lamb for the burnt offering, my son." And the two of them went on together. When they reached the place, God had told him about, Abraham built an altar there and arranged the wood on it. He bound his son Isaac and laid him on the altar, on top of the wood. Then he reached out his hand and took the knife to slay his son. But the angel of the Lord called out to him from heaven, "Abraham! Abraham!" "Here I am," he replied. "Do not lay a hand on the boy," he said. "Do not do anything to him. Now I know that you fear God, because you have not withheld from me your son, your only son."

Abraham looked up and there in a thicket he saw a ram caught by its horns. He went over and took the ram and sacrificed it as a burnt offering instead of his son. So, Abraham called that place The Lord Will Provide. And to this day it is said, "On the mountain of the Lord it will be provided." The angel of the Lord called to Abraham from heaven a second time and said, "I swear by myself, declares the Lord, that because you have done this and have not withheld your son, your only son, I will surely bless you and make your descendants as numerous as the stars in the sky and as the sand on the seashore. Your descendants will take possession of the cities of their enemies, and through your offspring all nations on earth will be blessed, because you have obeyed me." [Genesis 22:1-18 NIV]

The Promises of the Lord to Abraham:

The Lord placed Himself under a promise and made promises that He would fulfill on behalf of Abraham, from the call and blessing to the separation and blessing, the Lord said "I will" seven times to make the promises to Abraham and from the oath and blessing to the testing and blessing, the Lord said "I" in variance of "am, will, swear, know, remain, and give" also seven time to Abraham in certainty of the promises to him, the promises were; [Genesis 15:1-21, 22:1-18 NIV]

- *To make of Abraham a **great nation**. [Genesis 12:2 MEV]*
- *To **bless** Abraham. [Genesis 12:2 MEV]*
- *To make his **name great**, so that he will be a **blessing**. [Genesis 12:2 MEV]*
- *To **bless** those who bless Abraham and **curse** him who curses Abraham. [Genesis 12:3 MEV]*
- *To **bless** all **families** of the earth through Abraham. [Genesis 12:3 MEV]*
- *To **give** the land that Abraham saw to his descendants forever. [Genesis 13:15 MEV]*
- *To make Abraham's descendants like the dust of the earth, so that if a man could number the dust of the earth, then Abraham's descendants could also be numbered. [Genesis 13:16 MEV]*
- *To be Abraham's **shield**, and **very great reward**. [Genesis 15:1 NIV]*
- *To **give** him a son of his own **flesh** and **blood** to be his **heir**. [Genesis 15:4 NIV]*
- *To surely bless Abraham and his descendants, making them as numerous as the stars in the sky and as the sand on the seashore because Abraham did not withhold his only son from the Lord but was willing to offer him to the Lord. [Genesis 22:17 NIV]*
- *To make Abraham's descendants to **take possession** of cities of their enemies and through his offspring all nations on earth would be blessed. [Genesis 22:17-18 NIV]*

The greatest acts of Abraham before the Lord:

- *Obedience to God. He willingly obeyed the word of the Lord. [Genesis 22:18 NIV]*
- *Believing God, and God credited it to him as righteousness. [Genesis 15:67 NIV]*
- *Willingness to Sacrifice his only son he loves. [Genesis 22:8 NIV]*

"When God made His promise to Abraham, because He could vow by no one greater, He vowed by Himself, saying, "Surely I will bless you, and surely I will multiply you." So, after Abraham had patiently endured, he obtained the promise. For men indeed swear by a greater authority than themselves, and for them an oath of confirmation ends all dispute and argument. So, God, wanting to show more abundantly the immutability of His counsel to the heirs of promise, confirmed it by an oath (God wanted to make the unchanging nature of His purpose very clear to the heirs of what was promised, He confirmed it with an oath). So that by two immutable and unchangeable things, in which it was impossible for God to lie, we who have fled for refuge to take hold of the hope might have strong and great encouragement to hold fast to the hope set before us." [Hebrews 6:13-18 NIV]

"By faith Abraham, when God tested him, offered Isaac as a sacrifice. He who had embraced the promises was about to sacrifice his one and only son, even though God had said to him, "It is through Isaac that your offspring will be reckoned." Abraham reasoned that God could even raise the dead, and so in a manner of speaking he did receive Isaac back from death." [Hebrews 11:17-19 NIV]

The Principles-

- *Abraham was chosen and blessed by God through His covenant promise. [Genesis 15:5 NIV]*
- *God placed Himself under oath to fulfill His promises to Abraham. [Hebrews 6:13 ISV]*
- *God Himself will provide the lamb for the burnt offering, The Lord will provide, on the mountain of the Lord it will be provided. [Gen 22:8,14 NIV]*
- *Abraham believed God. [Genesis 15:6 NIV]*
- *Abraham was credited with righteousness by his faith in God. [Genesis 15:6 NIV]*

CHAPTER THREE

The Generation to Generations

In the moments of time, God was now about to begin fulfilling His promise and covenant to Abraham. God would begin to go through a series of events and encounters along the paths of life's journey in order to come true on His promises to Abraham. He begins the process from Abraham's third generation.

In Egypt.

- *Joseph:*

A seventeen-year-old shepherd by name Joseph, a loved son of Jacob, the son of Isaac, the son of Abraham had a dream at night. In this dream, He said; *""Listen to this dream I had: We were binding sheaves of grain out in the field when suddenly my sheaf rose and stood upright, while your sheaves gathered around mine and bowed down to it." [Genesis 37:6-7 NIV]*

He had another dream and it was same as the first; *""Listen," he said, "I had another dream, and this time the sun and moon and eleven stars were bowing down to me." [Genesis 37:9 NIV]*

He told these dreams to his father and brothers, whiles his father rebuked him, his brothers hated him more and more.

""Do you intend to reign over us? Will you actually rule us?" And they, his brothers, hated him all the more because of his dream and what he had said. His father rebuked him and said, "What is this dream you had? Will your mother and I and your brothers actually come and bow down to the ground before you?" His brothers were jealous of him, but his father kept the matter in mind." [Genesis 37:8, 10-11 NIV]

One day as he was sent to go and see the welfare of his brothers, they plotted to kill him as they said, *"here comes that dreamer!, the master of dreams comes!", [Genesis 37:19 NIV]* they had schemed to kill and place him in a cistern, after which they would fabricate a word about his death to their father, that a ferocious animal had devoured him. By the plans of the divine God, his elder brother Reuben heard this and tried to rescue him from their hands, he said to them; *"Let's not take his life, don't shed any blood. Throw him into this cistern here in the wilderness, but don't lay a hand on him." [Genesis 37:22 NIV]* In the minds of Reuben he had wanted to take him back to his father. Joseph's brothers stripped him of his ornate robe and threw him into the empty cistern, as time passed a caravan of Ishamaelites coming from Gilead, with camels loaded with spices, balm and myrrh on their way to Egypt passed by their route, so Judah said to his brothers, *"What will we gain if we kill our brother and cover up his blood? Come, let's sell him to the Ishmaelites and not lay our hands on him; after all, he is our brother, our own flesh and blood." [Genesis 37:26 NIV]* His brothers agreed with him and Joseph was sold to the Midianite merchants for twenty shekels of silver, the merchants took their brother to Egypt. When the Midianites reached Egypt, they sold Joseph to Potiphar, one of the official captains of the guards of Pharaoh.

In all the actions of the brothers, little did they know that they were under the divine hand of God to fulfill his promise and covenant He had with their great grandfather; Abraham. It was an act of God to place and position his divine purposes and plans into motion. The young man went to the house of Potiphar, one of Pharaoh's official, a captain of the guard, and since God was with him and fulfilling His purposes through him, he prospered in everything he did. When Joseph was in the household of his Egyptian master, Potiphar because the Lord was with him, he prospered in there to the extent that the master noticed that the Lord was with him and gave him success in everything he did, this caused Joseph to find favor in his eyes, becoming his personal attendant. Joseph became the manager in charge of his master's household and over all that the captain owned. He took care of everything both in the field and in the house for his master, the master had no care or concern for anything except this food to eat. It seems in the eyes of the Lord, Joseph was becoming too comfortable in the house of Potiphar, and the dream for which because he was sold was been neglected, so how does He get him to move to the next phase of his dream development? An incident would trigger a change in position in the life of this young man. His master's wife took notice of his handsomeness and natural well-built structure, this Joseph whom the Lord is with and built in physic has now become the center of attraction of his master's wife's desires. But he would not give in because of the fear for his God.

She said to him, *"Come to bed with me!" [Genesis 39:7 NIV]* the young Joseph fearing God refused and told her, *"my master does not concern himself with anything in the house; everything he owns he has entrusted to my care. No one is greater in this house than I am. My master has withheld nothing from me except you, because you are his wife. How then could I do such a wicked thing and sin against God?" [Genesis 39:8-9 NIV]* The woman persisted to no avail so she acted against him and when it did not work, told a lie about it to her husband which landed the young man into prison, this scheme of deception was put in place, unaware that it was leading to the fulfillment of the purpose of God; *"though she spoke to Joseph day after day, he refused to go to bed with her or even be with her. One day he went into the house to attend to his duties, and none of the household servants was inside. She caught him by his cloak and said, "Come to bed with me!" But he left his cloak in her hand and ran out of the house. When she saw that he had left his cloak in her hand and had run out of the house, she called her household servants. "Look," she said to them, "this Hebrew has been brought to us to make sport of us! He came in here to sleep with me, but I screamed. When he heard me scream for help, he left his cloak beside me and ran out of the house." She kept his cloak beside her until his master came home. Then she told him this story: "That Hebrew slave you brought us came to me to make sport of me. But as soon as I screamed for help, he left his cloak beside me and ran out of the house." When his master heard the story his wife told him, saying, "This is how your slave treated me," he burned with anger. Joseph's master took him and put him in prison, the place where the king's prisoners were confined. But while Joseph was there in the prison, the Lord was with him; he showed him kindness and granted him favor in the eyes of the prison warden. So, the warden put Joseph in charge of all those held in the prison, and he was made responsible for all that was done there. The warden paid no attention to anything under Joseph's care, because the Lord was with Joseph and gave him success in whatever he did."* [Genesis 39:10-23 NIV]

In the prison, his God was still with him to an extent that he became the one in charge of prisoners, since he prospered in everything he did. A chief cupbearer and a chief baker of the king of Egypt offended their master Pharaoh, Pharaoh being angry with them placed them in custody in the house of the captain of the guard in the same prison where Joseph was in confinement. Joseph became the attendant to these two chiefs; with time the cupbearer and the baker had a dream the same night and each person's dream had its own meaning. *[Genesis 40:1-6 NIV]* As usual, in the next morning as Joseph was attending to them, he saw their dejection and asked them, *"Why do you look so sad today?"* [Genesis 40:7 NIV] they answered him *"We both had dreams, but there is no one to interpret them."* [Genesis 40:8 NIV] Joseph gracefully asked and said to them, *"Do not interpretations belong to God? Tell me your dreams."* [Genesis 40:8 NIV] The chief cupbearer was the one to tell Joseph his dream first, he said, *"In my dream I saw a vine in front of me, and on the vine were three branches. As soon as it budded, it blossomed, and its clusters ripened into grapes. Pharaoh's cup was in my hand, and I took the grapes, squeezed them into Pharaoh's cup and put the cup in his hand."* [Genesis 40:9-11 NIV] Joseph went ahead to tell him the meaning of his dream, *"The three branches are three days. Within three days Pharaoh will lift up your head and restore you to your position, and you will put Pharaoh's cup in his hand, just as you used to do when you were his cupbearer."* [Genesis 40:12-13 NIV] As everybody in Joseph's situation would do, he asked for recommendation of kindness from the chief cupbearer to Pharaoh upon his release from the prison and when everything goes well with him, that the chief cupbearer could mention him to Pharaoh and get him out of the prison, even going ahead to tell him the story of how he was forcibly carried off from the Hebrews land into Egypt and also been placed in a dungeon for having done nothing deserving of such treatment. The chief baker when he heard the favorable interpretation expected same for his dream, he said, *"I too had a dream: On my head were three baskets of bread. In the top basket were all kinds of baked goods for Pharaoh, but the birds were eating them out of the basket on my head." [Genesis 40:16-17NIV]* Once again, Joseph gave him the true meaning to the dream, *"The three baskets are three days. Within three days Pharaoh will lift off your head and impale your body on a pole. And the birds will eat away your flesh." [Genesis 40:18-19 NIV]*

Since interpretation belongs to God, every meaning of dream of which Joseph gave to the two chiefs came to past, the three days after the dreams were the birthday of Pharaoh and he had a feast for all his officials, the heads of the chief cupbearer and chief baker were both lifted in the presence of the officials, whiles he restored the chief cup bearer to his original position, such that he again put the cup in the hand of Pharaoh, he impaled the chief baker according to the interpretation given by Joseph. But the chief cupbearer forgot to show kindness to Joseph and mention him to Pharaoh yet the God of all flesh was not done yet, He was not limited by man's forgetfulness. So now He made the king of Egypt himself to dream dreams so that the final piece of the puzzle could be set in place, fulfilling the first part of the grand purpose of God. God is about fulfilling His purpose so the chiefs of the king must be placed in prison and must have dreams, so that the master dreamer can interpret them, the master dreamer interprets their dreams and they are fulfilled. Now the dream of the dreamer must also be fulfilled, hence the Lord reveals to the king of the land the impending state of the world. All his *diviners,* could not reveal the meaning, calling for the dreamer to be brought in. *"When two full years had passed, Pharaoh had a dream: He was standing by the Nile, when out of the river there came up seven cows, sleek and fat, and they grazed among the reeds. After them, seven other cows, ugly and gaunt, came up out of the Nile and stood beside those on the riverbank. And the cows that were ugly and gaunt ate up the seven sleek, fat cows.*

Then Pharaoh woke up. He fell asleep again and had a second dream: Seven heads of grain, healthy and good, were growing on a single stalk. After them, seven other heads of grain sprouted—thin and scorched by the east wind. The thin heads of grain swallowed up the seven healthy, full heads. Then Pharaoh woke up; it had been a dream. In the morning his mind was troubled, so he sent for all the magicians and wise men of Egypt. Pharaoh told them his dreams, but no one could interpret them for him. Then the chief cupbearer said to Pharaoh, "Today I am reminded of my shortcomings. Pharaoh was once angry with his servants, and he imprisoned me and the chief baker in the house of the captain of the guard. Each of us had a dream the same night, and each dream had a meaning of its own. Now a young Hebrew was there with us, a servant of the captain of the guard. We told him our dreams, and he interpreted them for us, giving each man the interpretation of his dream. And things turned out exactly as he interpreted them to us: I was restored to my position, and the other man was impaled." So, Pharaoh sent for Joseph, and he was quickly brought from the dungeon. When he had shaved and changed his clothes, he came before Pharaoh. Pharaoh said to Joseph, "I had a dream, and no one can interpret it.

But I have heard it said of you that when you hear a dream you can interpret it." "I cannot do it," Joseph replied to Pharaoh, "but God will give Pharaoh the answer he desires."

Then Pharaoh said to Joseph, "In my dream I was standing on the bank of the Nile, when out of the river there came up seven cows, fat and sleek, and they grazed among the reeds. After them, seven other cows came up—scrawny and very ugly and lean. I had never seen such ugly cows in all the land of Egypt. The lean, ugly cows ate up the seven fat cows that came up first.

But even after they ate them, no one could tell that they had done so; they looked just as ugly as before. Then I woke up. "In my dream I saw seven heads of grain, full and good, growing on a single stalk. After them, seven other heads sprouted—withered and thin and scorched by the east wind. The thin heads of grain swallowed up the seven good heads. I told this to the magicians, but none of them could explain it to me." Then Joseph said to Pharaoh, "The dreams of Pharaoh are one and the same. God has revealed to Pharaoh what he is about to do. The seven good cows are seven years, and the seven good heads of grain are seven years; it is one and the same dream. The seven lean, ugly cows that came up afterward are seven years, and so are the seven worthless heads of grain scorched by the east wind: They are seven years of famine.

"It is just as I said to Pharaoh: God has shown Pharaoh what he is about to do. Seven years of great abundance are coming throughout the land of Egypt, but seven years of famine will follow them. Then all the abundance in Egypt will be forgotten, and the famine will ravage the land. The abundance in the land will not be remembered, because the famine that follows it will be so severe. The reason the dream was given to Pharaoh in two forms is that the matter has been firmly decided by God, and God will do it soon. "And now let Pharaoh look for a discerning and wise man and put him in charge of the land of Egypt. Let Pharaoh appoint commissioners over the land to take a fifth of the harvest of Egypt during the seven years of abundance. They should collect all the food of these good years that are coming and store up the grain under the authority of Pharaoh, to be kept in the cities for food.

This food should be held in reserve for the country, to be used during the seven years of famine that will come upon Egypt, so that the country may not be ruined by the famine." The plan seemed good to Pharaoh and to all his officials. So, Pharaoh asked them, "Can we find anyone like this man, one in whom is the spirit of God?" Then Pharaoh said to Joseph, "Since God has made all this known to you, there is no one so discerning and wise as you. You shall be in charge of my palace, and all my people are to submit to your orders. Only with respect to the throne will I be greater than you." Joseph in Charge of Egypt. So, Pharaoh said to Joseph, "I hereby put you in charge of the whole land of Egypt." Then Pharaoh took his signet ring from his finger and put it on Joseph's finger. He dressed him in robes of fine linen and put a gold chain around his neck. He had him ride in a chariot as his second-in-command, and people shouted before him, "Make way!" Thus, he put him in charge of the whole land of Egypt. Then Pharaoh said to Joseph, "I am Pharaoh, but without your word no one will lift hand or foot in all Egypt." Pharaoh gave Joseph the name Zaphenath-Paneah and gave him Asenath daughter of Potiphera, priest of On, to be his wife. And Joseph went throughout the land of Egypt. Joseph was thirty years old when he entered the service of Pharaoh king of Egypt. And Joseph went out from Pharaoh's presence and traveled throughout Egypt. During the seven years of abundance the land produced plentifully. Joseph collected all the food produced in those seven years of abundance in Egypt and stored it in the cities. In each city he put the food grown in the fields surrounding it. Joseph stored up huge quantities of grain, like the sand of the sea; it was so much that he stopped keeping records because it was beyond measure.

Before the years of famine came, two sons were born to Joseph by Asenath daughter of Potiphera, priest of On. Joseph named his firstborn Manasseh and said, "It is because God has made me forget all my trouble and all my father's household." The second son he named Ephraim and said, "It is because God has made me fruitful in the land of my suffering." The seven years of abundance in Egypt came to an end, and the seven years of famine began, just as Joseph had said. There was famine in all the other lands, but in the whole land of Egypt there was food. When all Egypt began to feel the famine, the people cried to Pharaoh for food. Then Pharaoh told all the Egyptians, "Go to Joseph and do what he tells you." When the famine had spread over the whole country, Joseph opened all the storehouses and sold grain to the Egyptians, for the famine was severe throughout Egypt. And all the world came to Egypt to buy grain from Joseph, because the famine was severe everywhere." [Genesis 41:1-57 NIV]

Joseph became the one in charge of seeing to the implementation of the interpretation of the dream and; *"without his word nothing could be lifted in Egypt at that time and all the world came to Egypt." [Genesis 41:44 NIV]*

It was finally here and a part of God's purpose has been fulfilled and Joseph's family had to come to him and bow down before him, his sheaf was now risen and standing upright, such that their sheaves must gather around his and bowed down to it, the time for the sun and moon and eleven stars to bow down to him had arrived. All these events happened for the dream he dreamt to be fulfilled, which was also a fulfillment of the Lord's promise to his grandfather, that his descendants would be strangers in a foreign land.

Now famine had taken over the world at the time the economy was on melt down, Jacob learned of the abundance of grain in Egypt, so he instructed his sons to go there and buy grain for the household *"so that we may live and not die."[Genesis 42:2 NIV]* At the instruction of their father, the ten brothers of Joseph went into Egypt to buy grain leaving behind their younger brother Benjamin, this was due to the father's fear that harm may come to his son from his beloved dead wife. When the brothers came to Egypt and since Joseph was the governor of the land and the person who sold grain to all people, they had to meet him, upon meeting him they bowed down to him with their faces to the ground, Joseph did recognize his brothers but pretended otherwise as a stranger and harshly spoke to them. He questioned where they were from and the reason for their coming to the land of Ham, accusing them of being spies sent to see the unprotected land of Egypt. Even though he knew them fully well, yet he tested them by requesting they bring to him their younger brother Benjamin, who was left home so as to verify the honesty of their word. He even placed them in custody for three days and repeated the same option to them on the third day, *"Do this and you will live, for I fear God: If you are honest men, let one of your brothers stay here in prison, while the rest of you go and take grain back for your starving households. But you must bring your youngest brother to me, so that your words may be verified and that you may not die." [Genesis 42:18-23 NIV]*

They then agreed to do as demanded of them by the pretending strange brother they had plotted to kill but later sold, the master dreamer they sort to eliminate. They said to one another, *"Surely we are being punished because of our brother. We saw how distressed he was when he pleaded with us for his life, but we would not listen; that's why this distress has come on us." Reuben replied, "Didn't I tell you not to sin against the boy? But you wouldn't listen! Now we must give an accounting for his blood." [Genesis 42:21-22 NIV]*

When they were saying all these, Joseph understood them but they did not realize so because he was using an interpreter. He kept Simeon, been bound and then ordered that their bags be filled with grain and for each man, their silver be replaced in his sack whiles being given provisions for their journey. On their way home they saw their silvers in the mouth of their sack as they stopped to feed their donkeys one night, this made their hearts sank and they trembled questioning themselves, *"What is this that God has done to us?" [Genesis 42:28 NIV]* they narrated their ordeal in the land of Egypt to their father when they arrived and told their father of the demand of the man who is lord over the land, *"This is how I will know whether you are honest men: Leave one of your brothers here with me, and take food for your starving households and go. But bring your youngest brother to me so I will know that you are not spies but honest men. Then I will give your brother back to you, and you can trade in the land."' [Genesis 42:33-34 NIV]*

Their father became frightened by all their words, including the pouch of silver that they all came back with, he said to them, *"You have deprived me of my children. Joseph is no more and Simeon is no more, and now you want to take Benjamin. Everything is against me!" [Genesis 42:36 NIV]*

Even after Reuben had assured the father that he would bring back his brother Benjamin should he be permitted to send him to the lord of the land, his father still would not allow it to be so, even though he says, *"You may put both of my sons to death if I do not bring him back to you. Entrust him to my care, and I will bring him back." [Genesis 42:37 NIV]* In response Jacob said, *"My son will not go down there with you; his brother is dead and he is the only one left. If harm comes to him on the journey you are taking, you will bring my gray head down to the grave in sorrow." [Genesis 42:38 NIV]*

But as the days went by and the famine was till severe, with all they had brought from Egypt finished, Jacob gave in and asked that they go back to Egypt for more food, *"Go back and buy us a little more food." [Genesis 43:2 NIV]* At this point Judah reminded their father, the words of the governor of the land of Ham, *"The man warned us solemnly, 'You will not see my face again unless your brother is with you.' If you will send our brother along with us, we will go down and buy food for you. But if you will not send him, we will not go down, because the man said to us, 'You will not see my face again unless your brother is with you.'" [Genesis 43:3-5 NIV]*

Israel, their father was troubled by the fact that his young son would be going to meet and be at the mercy of an unknown strange powerful man, but Judah said to Israel his father, *"Send the boy along with me and we will go at once, so that we and you and our children may live and not die. I myself will guarantee his safety; you can hold me personally responsible for him. If I do not bring him back to you and set him here before you, I will bear the blame before you all my life. As it is, if we had not delayed, we could have gone and returned twice."* [Genesis 43:8-10 NIV]

Their father Israel after a period of persuasion and assurances from his sons then agreed and said to them, *"If it must be, then do this: Put some of the best products of the land in your bags and take them down to the man as a gift —a little balm and a little honey, some spices and myrrh, some pistachio nuts and almonds. Take double the amount of silver with you, for you must return the silver that was put back into the mouths of your sacks. Perhaps it was a mistake. Take your brother also and go back to the man at once. And may God Almighty grant you mercy before the man so that he will let your other brother and Benjamin come back with you. As for me, if I am bereaved, I am bereaved."* [Genesis 43:11-14 NIV]

The brothers took gifts as suggested by their father and double the amount of silver along with Benjamin, they went down on their way to Egypt to present themselves to Joseph.

Upon seeing his brothers with their younger brother, Joseph asked the steward to, *"Take these men to my house, slaughter an animal and prepare a meal; they are to eat with me at noon."* [Genesis 43:16 NIV] As the steward of the house of his master, he obliged accordingly even though the sons of Israel were frightened as they were taken into the house, they thought, *"We were brought here because of the silver that was put back into our sacks the first time. He wants to attack us and overpower us and seize us as slaves and take our donkeys."* So, they went up to Joseph's steward and spoke to him at the entrance to the house. *"We beg your pardon, our lord,"* they said, *"We came down here the first time to buy food. But at the place where we stopped for the night, we opened our sacks and each of us found his silver—the exact weight—in the mouth of his sack. So, we have brought it back with us. We have also brought additional silver with us to buy food. We don't know who put our silver in our sacks."* *"It's all right,"* he said. *"Don't be afraid. Your God, the God of your father, has given you treasure in your sacks; I received your silver."* Then he brought Simeon out to them. [Genesis 43:20-23 NIV]

The steward attended to them in the house of Joseph, giving them water to wash their feet, provided them with fodder for their donkeys as they prepared their gifts for the arrival of Joseph because they were to eat there with him. They presented their gifts as they have prepared when Joseph arrived, he asked about their father, *"How is your aged father you told me about? Is he still living?"* [Genesis 43:27 NIV] The brothers replied to him, *"Your servant our father is still alive and well."* [Genesis 43:28 NIV] Joseph looked about and saw his brother Benjamin, his own mother's son, so he asked, *"Is this your youngest brother, the one you told me about?"* And he said, *"God be gracious to you, my son."* Deeply moved at the sight of his brother, Joseph hurried out and looked for a place to weep. He went into his private room and wept there. After he had washed his face, he came out and, controlling himself, said, *"Serve the food."* They served him by himself, the brothers by themselves, *and the Egyptians who ate with him by themselves, because Egyptians could not eat with Hebrews, for that is detestable to Egyptians. The men had been seated before him in the order of their ages, from the firstborn to the youngest; and they looked at each other in astonishment. When portions were served to them from Joseph's table, Benjamin's portion was five times as much as anyone else's. So, they feasted and drank freely with him."* [Genesis 43:29-34 NIV]

After the meal, Joseph made himself known to his brothers because he could no longer control himself whiles weeping loudly, to an extent that the household of Pharaoh heard about it, that Joseph had been reunited with his brothers, He inquired about this father; *"I am Joseph! Is my father still living?"* [Genesis 45:3 NIV] This brother out of fear and terror would not answer him, so he said to them; *"Come close to me."* [Genesis 45:4 NIV] When they did that he insisted to them that he was their younger brother, the one they sold into Egypt, urging them not to be distressed and angry with themselves for their actions because; *"it was to save lives that God sent me ahead of you. For two years now there has been famine in the land, and for the next five years there will be no plowing and reaping. But God sent me ahead of you to preserve for you a remnant on earth and to save your lives by a great deliverance. "So, then, it was not you who sent me here, but God. He made me father to Pharaoh, lord of his entire household and ruler of all Egypt."* [Genesis 45:7-8 NIV] Upon this revelation to his brothers and the impeding famine in all the lands, all of the household of Jacob came to Egypt and settled in the land of Ham in the area of Goshen. *[Genesis 46:1-34 NIV]*

The Stages of Purpose Fulfillment for Joseph: [Genesis 37, 39 NIV]

- *In the father's house, he receives a dream from the Lord about the assignment for his life and the future destiny of his family, he needs to be prepared and made ready for the assignment and counsel of the Lord. [Genesis 37:1,5 and 9 NIV]*

   So, the Lord must send him into a foreign land, a land unpopular and unusual, his brothers must be the means to allow God's plan to be fulfilled. He is sold as a slave bound by chains and fitters. [Genesis 37:28 NIV]

- *In Potiphar's house, he is now a slave in a foreign land, he prospers and is placed in charge of his master's household, still under the "furnace of refinery" of the Lord. The time is not yet up, things must cause him to move to the next stage of the process. He is lied upon and thrown into the king's prison. [Genesis 39:1-4 NIV]*
- *In Prison: it is time for prison, another place for further training to prepare him, now the time of the prediction is near, the word of the Lord has fully refined him. [Genesis 39:20 NIV]*
- *In the Palace, God now causes a world famine, sends a king to release him, makes him a ruler of his people and sets him free. He is made the master over his household, the manager of all his possessions- to discipline his rulers at will and make his elders wise. Ultimately God made*

> *Joseph a father to Pharaoh. Now all is set, Jacob goes to Egypt and God's promise to Abraham is set with others yet to follow. [Genesis 39:39-40 NIV]*

The Principles-

- *God fulfills His purposes in processes and stages of time.*
- *God fulfills His purposes in places and times.*
- *God fulfills His purposes with and through peoples.*
- *God works all things for the good of His purpose.*
- *God moves in the affairs of man.*

"Now, do not be distressed and do not be angry with yourselves for selling me here, because it was to save lives that God sent me ahead of you." – Joseph to the brothers. [Genesis 45:5 NIV]

All this was to fulfill God's promise to Abraham as He made a covenant to him, making him know that a time would come where his descendants would be strangers and under bondage in a foreign land until the people of the land of heritage's sin had reached its full measure. As time went by, it was time for God to bring the next phase of His purpose into effect. Israel had increased and become a great nation in Egypt, and again for God to fulfill His purpose and plan, a new king arose to set the course into motion. *"Israelites were exceedingly fruitful; they multiplied greatly, increased in numbers and became so numerous that the land was filled with them. Then a new king, to whom Joseph meant nothing, came to power in Egypt. "Look," he said to his people, "the Israelites have become far too numerous for us. Come, we must deal shrewdly with them or they will become even more numerous and, if war breaks out, will join our enemies, fight against us and leave the country." So, they put slave masters over them to oppress them with forced labor, and they built Pithom and Rameses as store cities for Pharaoh. But the more they were oppressed, the more they multiplied and spread; so, the Egyptians came to dread the Israelites and worked them ruthlessly. They made their lives bitter with harsh labor in brick and mortar and with all kinds of work in the fields; in all their harsh labor the Egyptians worked them ruthlessly. The king of Egypt said to the Hebrew midwives, whose names were Shiphrah and Puah, "When you are helping the Hebrew women during childbirth on the delivery stool, if you see that the baby is a boy, kill him; but if it is a girl, let her live." The midwives, however, feared God and did not do what the king of Egypt had told them to do; they let the boys live. Then the king of Egypt summoned the midwives and asked them, "Why have you done this? Why have you let the boys live?" The midwives answered Pharaoh, "Hebrew women are not like Egyptian women; they are vigorous and give birth before the midwives arrive."*

So, God was kind to the midwives and the people increased and became even more numerous. And because the midwives feared God, he gave them families of their own. Then Pharaoh gave this order

to all his people: "Every Hebrew boy that is born you must throw into the Nile, but let every girl live."
[Exodus 1:7-22 NIV]

It was during this period of time that God set his next phase of covenant fulfillment in place. A child was born;

- *Moses:*

"Now a man of the tribe of Levi married a Levite woman, and she became pregnant and gave birth to a son. When she saw that he was a fine child, she hid him for three months. But when she could hide him no longer, she got a papyrus basket for him and coated it with tar and pitch. Then she placed the child in it and put it among the reeds along the bank of the Nile. His sister stood at a distance to see what would happen to him. Then Pharaoh's daughter went down to the Nile to bathe, and her attendants were walking along the riverbank. She saw the basket among the reeds and sent her female slave to get it. She opened it and saw the baby. He was crying, and she felt sorry for him. "This is one of the Hebrew babies," she said. Then his sister asked Pharaoh's daughter, "Shall I go and get one of the Hebrew women to nurse the baby for you?" "Yes, go," she answered. So, the girl went and got the baby's mother. Pharaoh's daughter said to her, "Take this baby and nurse him for me, and I will pay you." So, the woman took the baby and nursed him. When the child grew older, she took him to Pharaoh's daughter and he became her son. She named him Moses, saying, "I drew him out of the water."

One day, after Moses had grown up, he went out to where his own people were and watched them at their hard labor. He saw an Egyptian beating a Hebrew, one of his own people. Looking this way and that and seeing no one, he killed the Egyptian and hid him in the sand. The next day he went out and saw two Hebrews fighting. He asked the one in the wrong, "Why are you hitting your fellow Hebrew?" The man said, "Who made you ruler and judge over us? Are you thinking of killing me as you killed the Egyptian?" Then Moses was afraid and thought, "What I did must have become known." When Pharaoh heard of this, he tried to kill Moses, but Moses fled from Pharaoh and went to live in Midian, where he sat down by a well. Now a priest of Midian had seven daughters, and they came to draw water and fill the troughs to water their father's flock. Some shepherds came along and drove them away, but Moses got up and came to their rescue and watered their flock.

When the girls returned to Reuel their father, he asked them, "Why have you returned so early today?" They answered, "An Egyptian rescued us from the shepherds. He even drew water for us and watered the flock." "And, where is he?" Reuel asked his daughters. "Why did you leave him? Invite him to have something to eat." Moses agreed to stay with the man, who gave his daughter Zipporah to Moses in marriage. Zipporah gave birth to a son, and Moses named him Gershom, saying, "I have become a foreigner in a foreign land."

During that long period, the king of Egypt died. The Israelites groaned in their slavery and cried out, and their cry for help because of their slavery went up to God. God heard their groaning and he remembered his covenant with Abraham, with Isaac and with Jacob. So, God looked on the Israelites and was concerned about them.

Now Moses was tending the flock of Jethro his father-in-law, the priest of Midian, and he led the flock to the far side of the wilderness and came to Horeb, the mountain of God. There the angel of the Lord appeared to him in flames of fire from within a bush. Moses saw that though the bush was on fire it did not burn up. So, Moses thought, "I will go over and see this strange sight—why the bush does not burn up."

When the Lord saw that he had gone over to look, God called to him from within the bush, "Moses! Moses!" And Moses said, "Here I am." "Do not come any closer," God said. "Take off your sandals, for the place where you are standing is holy ground." Then he said, "I am the God of your father, the God of Abraham, the God of Isaac and the God of Jacob." At this, Moses hid his face, because he was afraid to look at God. The Lord said, "I have indeed seen the misery of my people in Egypt. I have heard them crying out because of their slave drivers, and I am concerned about their suffering. So, I have come down to rescue them from the hand of the Egyptians and to bring them up out of that land into a good and spacious land, a land flowing with milk and honey —the home of the Canaanites, Hittites, Amorites, Perizzites, Hivites and Jebusites. And now the cry of the Israelites has reached me, and I have seen the way the Egyptians are oppressing them. So now, go. I am sending you to Pharaoh to bring my people the Israelites out of Egypt." But Moses said to God, "Who am I that I should go to Pharaoh and bring the Israelites out of Egypt?" And God said, "I will be with you. And this will be the sign to you that it is I who have sent you: When you have brought the people out of Egypt, you will worship God on this mountain." Moses said to God, "Suppose I go to the Israelites and say to them,

'The God of your fathers has sent me to you,' and they ask me, 'What is his name?' Then what shall I tell them?" God said to Moses, "I am who I am. This is what you are to say to the Israelites: 'I am has sent me to you.'" God also said to Moses, "Say to the Israelites, 'The Lord, the God of your fathers — the God of Abraham, the God of Isaac and the God of Jacob —has sent me to you.' "This is my name forever, the name you shall call me from generation to generation. "Go, assemble the elders of Israel and say to them, 'The Lord, the God of your fathers—the God of Abraham, Isaac and Jacob —appeared to me and said: I have watched over you and have seen what has been done to you in Egypt. And I have promised to bring you up out of your misery in Egypt into the land of the Canaanites, Hittites, Amorites, Perizzites, Hivites and Jebusites—a land flowing with milk and honey.' "The elders of Israel will listen to you. Then you and the elders are to go to the king of Egypt and say to him, 'The Lord, the God of the Hebrews, has met with us. Let us take a three-day journey into the wilderness to offer sacrifices to the Lord our God.' But I know that the king of Egypt will not let you go unless a mighty hand compels him. So, I will stretch out my hand and strike the Egyptians with all the wonders that I will perform among them. After that, he will let you go.

"And I will make the Egyptians favorably disposed toward this people, so that when you leave you will not go empty-handed. Every woman is to ask her neighbor and any woman living in her house for *articles of silver and gold and for clothing, which you will put on your sons and daughters. And so, you will plunder the Egyptians."*

Signs for Moses: Moses answered, *"What if they do not believe me or listen to me and say, 'The Lord did not appear to you'?"*

Then the Lord said to him, "What is that in your hand?"

"A staff," he replied. The Lord said, "Throw it on the ground." Moses threw it on the ground and it became a snake, and he ran from it. Then the Lord said to him, "Reach out your hand and take it by the tail." So, Moses reached out and took hold of the snake and it turned back into a staff in his hand. "This," said the Lord, "is so that they may believe that the Lord, the God of their fathers—the God of Abraham, the God of Isaac and the God of Jacob—has appeared to you." Then the Lord said, "Put your hand inside your cloak." So, Moses put his hand into his cloak, and when he took it out, the skin was leprous—it had become as white as snow. "Now put it back into your cloak," he said. So, Moses put his hand back into his cloak, and when he took it out, it was restored, like the rest of his flesh.

Then the Lord said, "If they do not believe you or pay attention to the first sign, they may believe the second. But if they do not believe these two signs or listen to you, take some water from the Nile and pour it on the dry ground. The water you take from the river will become blood on the ground." Moses said to the Lord, "Pardon your servant, Lord. I have never been eloquent, neither in the past nor since you have spoken to your servant. I am slow of speech and tongue." The Lord said to him, "Who gave human beings their mouths? Who makes them deaf or mute? Who gives them sight or makes them blind? Is it not I, the Lord? Now go; I will help you speak and will teach you what to say." But Moses said, "Pardon your servant, Lord. Please send someone else." Then the Lord's anger burned against Moses and he said, "What about your brother, Aaron the Levite? I know he can speak well. He is already on his way to meet you, and he will be glad to see you. You shall speak to him and put words in his mouth; I will help both of you speak and will teach you what to do.

He will speak to the people for you, and it will be as if he were your mouth and as if you were God to him. But take this staff in your hand so you can perform the signs with it." Then Moses went back to Jethro his father-in-law and said to him, "Let me return to my own people in Egypt to see if any of them are still alive." Jethro said, "Go, and I wish you well." Now the Lord had said to Moses in Midian, "Go back to Egypt, for all those who wanted to kill you are dead." So, Moses took his wife and sons, put them on a donkey and started back to Egypt. And he took the staff of God in his hand. The Lord said to Moses, "When you return to Egypt, see that you perform before Pharaoh all the wonders I have given you the power to do. But I will harden his heart so that he will not let the people go. Then say to Pharaoh, 'This is what the Lord says: Israel is my firstborn son, and I told you, "Let my son go, so he may worship me." But you refused to let him go; so, I will kill your firstborn son.'" At a lodging place on the way, the Lord met Moses and was about to kill him. But Zipporah took a flint knife, cut off her son's foreskin and touched Moses' feet with it. "Surely you are a bridegroom of blood to me," she said. So, the Lord let him alone. (At that time, she said "bridegroom of blood," referring to circumcision.)

The Lord said to Aaron, "Go into the wilderness to meet Moses." So, he met Moses at the mountain of God and kissed him. Then Moses told Aaron everything the Lord had sent him to say, and also about all the signs he had commanded him to perform. Moses and Aaron brought together all the elders of the Israelites, and Aaron told them everything the Lord had said to Moses. He also performed the signs before the people, and they believed. And when they heard that the Lord was concerned about them and had seen their misery, they bowed down and worshiped." [Exodus 2:1-24, 3:1-22, 4:1-31 NIV]

The Stages of Purpose Fulfillment for Moses: [Exodus 1, 2 and 3 NIV]

- *Divine time of birth, a wicked decree was in place to kill all sons born during his time. Yet the wickedness of the decree would not limit the birth of Moses. God is not limited by human decrees. [Exodus 1:16 NIV]*
- *Divine position in life, being kept for three months after birth, he was now placed in the river Nile the very same time the daughter of the king was coming to bathe. [Exodus 2:1-5 NIV]*
- *Divine assistance of help, the daughter of Pharaoh takes him into the palace to train him according to divine counsel. [Exodus 2:10 NIV]*
- *Divine preparation, after an attempt to deliver justice to his people Moses had to be prepared with the sheep in the wilderness, in order to be able to lead the people as the shepherd, his preparation would take about forty years. [Exodus 3:1 NIV]*
- *Divine association, He meets the priest of the Lord and marries a daughter. His association was to be the wise counsel and the eyes he would need for his next journey of leadership and assignment fulfilment. [Exodus 2:21 NIV]*
- *Divine attraction, the time was now up and God needed his attention to bring him into the reason for his birth, a bush was on fire it did not burn up. So, Moses thought to himself and went over to see the strange sight he was seeing, this was the divine's way of attracting him and getting his attention for the next move. [Exodus 3:1-3 NIV]*
- *Divine assignment, the Lord had indeed seen the misery of His people and needed a deliverer, He had heard of the cry of the people due to the slave drivers and was concerned with their suffering, so He had come down to rescue His people from the hand of the Egyptians by the hand of Moses and to bring them up out of that land into a good and spacious land, a land flowing with milk and honey —the home of covenant promise to Abraham. Moses was now assigned with going to bring His people out! [Exodus 3:7-10 NIV]*
- *Divine accomplishment, every mission of man, requires a commission of God, the hand of God and the hand of man. Moses questioned God of who he was, that he was to go to the powerful Pharaoh and bring the Israelites out of Egypt but God told him, He was going to be with him, which would be the sign that He had commissioned him. [Exodus 3:11-12 NIV] He, the Lord sealed Moses with His name; "I am who I am. 'I am has sent me to you… This is my name*

forever, the name you shall call me from generation to generation." [Exodus 3:14 NIV] And with the staff in his hand He made onto him a weapon of power.

- *Divine ability, God was able to perform with him what he called him for. Moses' inability of not being eloquent was not an inability for the Lord, His slowness of tongue was never an issue for the Lord, the one who gives mouth to humans, the one who makes the deaf and mute, who gives sight and makes blind. [Exodus 4:1-4 NIV]*

The Principles-

- *Divine counsel positions.*
- *Divine counsel plans.*
- *Divine counsel prepares.*
- *Divine counsel performs.*
- *Divine counsel reveals.*
- *Divine counsel reigns.*

The divine counsel of the divine Godhead is positioned by plans, preparations and performances to reveal the reigns of the divine Godhead.

- *Pharaoh: signs and wonders.*

Pharaoh is the adversary, the king of Egypt that they must overcome. He is the opposition to the counsel and purposes of God. God hardened his heart to show His mighty power and make His name known. He seeks to challenge the power and might of the sovereign God to frustrate His plans and purposes. When Moses and Aaron went to him to declare the counsel of the LORD, the God of Israel *"Let My people go, that they may hold a feast [festival] to Me in the wilderness" [Exodus 5:1 NIV, MEV]* to him, in response; *"Pharaoh said, "Who is the Lord, that I should obey him and let Israel go? I do not know the Lord and I will not let Israel go. The king of Egypt said, "Moses and Aaron, why are you taking the people away from their labor? Get back to your work!" Then Pharaoh said, "Look, the people of the land are now numerous, and you are stopping them from working." That same day Pharaoh gave this order to the slave drivers and overseers in charge of the people: "You are no longer to supply the people with straw for making bricks; let them go and gather their own straw. But require them to make the same number of bricks as before; don't reduce the quota. They are lazy; that is why they are crying out, 'Let us go and sacrifice to our God.'*

Make the work harder for the people so that they keep working and pay no attention to lies." Then the slave drivers and the overseers went out and said to the people,

"This is what Pharaoh says: 'I will not give you any more straw. Go and get your own straw wherever you can find it, but your work will not be reduced at all.'" So, the people scattered all over Egypt to gather

stubble to use for straw. The slave drivers kept pressing them, saying, "Complete the work required of you for each day, just as when you had straw."

And Pharaoh's slave drivers beat the Israelite overseers they had appointed, demanding, "Why haven't you met your quota of bricks yesterday or today, as before?" Then the Israelite overseers went and appealed to Pharaoh: "Why have you treated your servants this way? Your servants are given no straw, yet we are told, 'Make bricks!' Your servants are being beaten, but the fault is with your own people." Pharaoh said, "Lazy, that's what you are—lazy! That is why you keep saying, 'Let us go and sacrifice to the Lord.' Now get to work. You will not be given any straw, yet you must produce your full quota of bricks."" [Exodus 5:2-14 NIV]

Instead of Pharaoh obeying the word of the Lord, he opposed it and increased the burden of the people of God, in effect he was telling God, I do not know you, I would not obey your word and I will inflict more burden on your people since you seek to deliver them from my rule. He rejected the choice of God and interfered with the plans of God for His people, he dejected and oppressed the people of God by slavery and bondage of servitude. God always has a reply to the resistance of Pharaoh, and it is superior.

"The Lord said to Moses, "Now you will see what I will do to Pharaoh: Because of my mighty hand he will let them go; because of my mighty hand he will drive them out of his country." God also said to Moses, "I am the Lord. I appeared to Abraham, to Isaac and to Jacob as God Almighty, but by my name the Lord I did not make myself fully known to them. I also established my covenant with them to give them the land of Canaan, where they resided as foreigners. Moreover, I have heard the groaning of the Israelites, whom the Egyptians are enslaving, and I have remembered my covenant. "Therefore, say to the Israelites: 'I am the Lord, and I will bring you out from under the yoke of the Egyptians. I will free you from being slaves to them, and I will redeem you with an outstretched arm and with mighty acts of judgment. I will take you as my own people, and I will be your God. Then you will know that I am the Lord your God, who brought you out from under the yoke of the Egyptians. And I will bring you to the land I swore with uplifted hand to give to Abraham, to Isaac and to Jacob. I will give it to you as a possession. I am the Lord.'" The Lord said to Moses, "Go, tell Pharaoh king of Egypt to let the Israelites go out of his country." [Exodus 6:1-8 NIV]

The Lord moved all this power into the current situation, He told Moses to *now* observe what He would do to Pharaoh by His mighty hand, by His mighty hand He was going to cause Pharaoh to drive out the Lord's people from Pharaoh's country. The Lord released His mighty hand to act on behalf of His people, to release His people from the yoke of the Egyptians, as the Lord who had appeared to their ancestors and made an oath covenant to their fathers, He was going to fully make Himself known to Pharaoh by His name. He had heard the groans of His people by their enslavement, He had remembered His covenant and was now coming to free them, redeem them by His outstretched arm as He had sworn by His uplifted hand to do and give them a land as their possession and heritage.

"Then the Lord said to Moses, "See, I have made you like God to Pharaoh, and your brother Aaron will be your prophet. You are to say everything I command you, and your brother Aaron is to tell Pharaoh to let the Israelites go out of his country. But I will harden Pharaoh's heart, and though I multiply my signs and wonders in Egypt, he will not listen to you. Then I will lay my hand on Egypt and with mighty acts of judgment I will bring out my divisions, my people the Israelites. And the Egyptians will know that I am the Lord when I stretch out my hand against Egypt and bring the Israelites out of it." Moses and Aaron did just as the Lord commanded them. Moses was eighty years old and Aaron eighty-three when they spoke to Pharaoh. The Lord said to Moses and Aaron, "When Pharaoh says to you, 'Perform a miracle,' then say to Aaron, 'Take your staff and throw it down before Pharaoh,' and it will become a snake." So, Moses and Aaron went to Pharaoh and did just as the Lord commanded. Aaron threw his staff down in front of Pharaoh and his officials, and it became a snake.

Pharaoh then summoned wise men and sorcerers, and the Egyptian magicians also did the same things by their secret arts: Each one threw down his staff and it became a snake. But Aaron's staff swallowed up their staffs.

Yet Pharaoh's heart became hard and he would not listen to them, just as the Lord had said. Then the Lord said to Moses, "Pharaoh's heart is unyielding; he refuses to let the people go. Go to Pharaoh in the morning as he goes out to the river. Confront him on the bank of the Nile, and take in your hand the staff that was changed into a snake. Then say to him, 'The Lord, the God of the Hebrews, has sent me to say to you: Let my people go, so that they may worship me in the wilderness. But until now you have not listened. This is what the Lord says: By this you will know that I am the Lord: With the staff that is in my hand I will strike the water of the Nile, and it will be changed into blood. The fish in the Nile will die, and the river will stink; the Egyptians will not be able to drink its water.'" The Lord said to Moses, "Tell Aaron, 'Take your staff and stretch out your hand over the waters of Egypt—over the streams and canals, over the ponds and all the reservoirs—and they will turn to blood.' Blood will be everywhere in Egypt, even in vessels of wood and stone." Moses and Aaron did just as the Lord had commanded. He raised his staff in the presence of Pharaoh and his officials and struck the water of the Nile, and all the water was changed into blood. The fish in the Nile died, and the river smelled so bad that the Egyptians could not drink its water. Blood was everywhere in Egypt. But the Egyptian magicians did the same things by their secret arts, and Pharaoh's heart became hard; he would not listen to Moses and Aaron, just as the Lord had said. Instead, he turned and went into his palace, and did not take even this to heart. And all the Egyptians dug along the Nile to get drinking water, because they could not drink the water of the river.

Seven days passed after the Lord struck the Nile. Then the Lord said to Moses,

"Go to Pharaoh and say to him, 'This is what the Lord says: Let my people go, so that they may worship me. If you refuse to let them go, I will send a plague of frogs on your whole country. The Nile will teem with frogs. They will come up into your palace and your bedroom and onto your bed, into the houses of your officials and on your people, and into your ovens and kneading troughs. The frogs will come up on you and your people and all your officials.'" Then the Lord said to Moses, "Tell Aaron, 'Stretch out your hand with your staff over the streams and canals and ponds, and make frogs come up on the land of Egypt.'" So, Aaron stretched out his hand over the waters of Egypt, and the frogs came up and covered the land. But the magicians did the same things by their secret arts; they also made frogs come up on the land of Egypt. Pharaoh summoned Moses and Aaron and said, "Pray to the Lord to take the frogs away from me and my people, and I will let your people go to offer sacrifices to the Lord." Moses said to Pharaoh, "I leave to you the honor of setting the time for me to pray for you and your officials and your people that you and your houses may be rid of the frogs, except for those that remain in the Nile." "Tomorrow," Pharaoh said. Moses replied, "It will be as you say, so that you may know there is no one like the Lord our God. The frogs will leave you and your houses, your officials and your people; they will remain only in the Nile." After Moses and Aaron left Pharaoh, Moses cried out to the Lord about the frogs he had brought on Pharaoh.

And the Lord did what Moses asked. The frogs died in the houses, in the courtyards and in the fields. They were piled into heaps, and the land reeked of them. But when Pharaoh saw that there was relief, he hardened his heart and would not listen to Moses and Aaron, just as the Lord had said.

Then the Lord said to Moses, "Tell Aaron, 'Stretch out your staff and strike the dust of the ground,' and throughout the land of Egypt the dust will become gnats." They did this, and when Aaron stretched out his hand with the staff and struck the dust of the ground, gnats came on people and animals. All the dust throughout the land of Egypt became gnats. But when the magicians tried to produce gnats by their secret arts, they could not. Since the gnats were on people and animals everywhere, the magicians said to Pharaoh, "This is the finger of God." But Pharaoh's heart was hard and he would not listen, just as the Lord had said. Then the Lord said to Moses, "Get up early in the morning and confront Pharaoh as he goes to the river and say to him, 'This is what the Lord says: Let my people go, so that they may worship me. If you do not let my people go, I will send swarms of flies on you and your officials, on your people and into your houses. The houses of the Egyptians will be full of flies; even the ground will be covered with them.

"'But on that day, I will deal differently with the land of Goshen, where my people live; no swarms of flies will be there, so that you will know that I, the Lord, am in this land. I will make a distinction between my people and your people. This sign will occur tomorrow.'" And the Lord did this. Dense swarms of flies poured into Pharaoh's palace and into the houses of his officials; throughout Egypt the land was ruined by the flies.

Then Pharaoh summoned Moses and Aaron and said, "Go, sacrifice to your God here in the land." But Moses said, "That would not be right. The sacrifices we offer the Lord our God would be detestable to the Egyptians. And if we offer sacrifices that are detestable in their eyes, will they not stone us? We must take a three-day journey into the wilderness to offer sacrifices to the Lord our God, as he commands us." Pharaoh said, "I will let you go to offer sacrifices to the Lord your God in the wilderness, but you must not go far. Now pray for me. So they took soot from a furnace and stood before Pharaoh. Moses tossed it *into the air, and festering boils broke out on people and animals. The magicians could not stand before Moses because of the boils that were on them and on all the Egyptians. But the Lord hardened Pharaoh's heart and he would not listen to Moses and Aaron, just as the Lord had said to Moses. Then the Lord said to Moses, "Get up early in the morning, confront Pharaoh and say to him, 'This is what the Lord, the God of the Hebrews, says: Let my people go, so that they may worship me, or this time I will send the full force of my plagues against you and against your officials and your people, so you may know that there is no one like me in all the earth. For by now I could have stretched out my hand and struck you and your people with a plague that would have wiped you off the earth. But I have raised you up for this very purpose, that I might show you my power and that my name might be proclaimed in all the earth. You still set yourself against my people and will not let them go. Therefore, at this time tomorrow I will send the worst hailstorm that has ever fallen on Egypt, from the day it was founded till now. Give an order now to bring your livestock and everything you have in the field to a place of shelter, because the hail will fall on every person and animal that has not been brought in and is still out in the field, and they will die.'" Those officials of Pharaoh who feared the word of the Lord hurried to bring their slaves and their livestock inside. But those who ignored the word of the Lord left their slaves and livestock in the field. Then the Lord said to Moses, "Stretch out your hand toward the sky so that hail will fall all over Egypt—on people and animals and on everything growing in the fields of Egypt." When Moses stretched out his staff toward the sky, the Lord sent thunder and hail, and lightning flashed down to the ground. So, the Lord rained hail on the land of Egypt; hail fell and lightning flashed back and forth. It was the worst storm in all the land of Egypt since it had become a nation. Throughout Egypt hail struck everything in the fields—both people and animals; it beat down everything growing in the fields and stripped every tree. The only place it did not hail was the land of Goshen, where the Israelites were. Then Pharaoh summoned Moses and Aaron. "This time I have sinned," he said to them. "The Lord is in the right, and I and my people are in the wrong. Pray to the Lord, for we have had enough thunder and hail. I will let you go; you don't have to stay any longer." Moses replied, "When I have gone out of the city, I will spread out my hands in prayer to the Lord. The thunder will stop and there will be no more hail, so you may know that the earth is the Lord's. But I know that you and your officials still do not fear the Lord God."*

(The flax and barley were destroyed, since the barley had headed and the flax was in bloom. The wheat and spelt, however, were not destroyed, because they ripen later.) Then Moses left Pharaoh and went out of the city. He spread out his hands toward the Lord; the thunder and hail stopped, and the rain no longer poured down on the land. When Pharaoh saw that the rain and hail and thunder had stopped, he sinned again: He and his officials hardened their hearts. So Pharaoh's heart was hard and he would not let the Israelites go, just as the Lord had said through Moses. Then the Lord said to Moses, "Go to Pharaoh, for I have hardened his heart and the hearts of his officials so that I may perform these signs of mine among them that you may tell your children and grandchildren how I dealt harshly with the Egyptians and how I performed my signs among them, and that you may know that I am the

Lord." So, Moses and Aaron went to Pharaoh and said to him, "This is what the Lord, the God of the Hebrews, says: 'How long will you refuse to humble yourself before me? Let my people go, so that they may worship me. If you refuse to let them go, I will bring locusts into your country tomorrow. They will cover the face of the ground so that it cannot be seen. They will devour what little you have left after the hail, including every tree that is growing in your fields. They will fill your houses and those of all your officials and all the Egyptians—something neither your parents nor your ancestors have ever seen from the day they settled in this land till now.'" Then Moses turned and left Pharaoh. Pharaoh's officials said to him, "How long will this man be a snare to us? Let the people go, so that they may worship the Lord their God. Do you not yet realize that Egypt is ruined?" Then Moses and Aaron were brought back to Pharaoh. "Go, worship the Lord your God," he said. "But tell me who will be going." Moses answered, "We will go with our young and our old, with our sons and our daughters, and with our flocks and herds, because we are to celebrate a festival to the Lord." Pharaoh said, "The Lord be with you—if I let you go, along with your women and children! Clearly you are bent on evil. No!

Have only the men gone and worship the Lord, since that's what you have been asking for." Then Moses and Aaron were driven out of Pharaoh's presence. And the Lord said to Moses, "Stretch out your hand over Egypt so that locusts swarm over the land and devour everything growing in the fields, everything left by the hail." So. Moses stretched out his staff over Egypt, and the Lord made an east wind blow across the land all that day and all that night. By morning the wind had brought the locusts; they invaded all Egypt and settled down in every area of the country in great numbers. Never before had there been such a plague of locusts, nor will there ever be again. They covered all the ground until it was black. They devoured all that was left after the hail—everything growing in the fields and the fruit on the trees. Nothing green remained on tree or plant in all the land of Egypt. Pharaoh quickly summoned Moses and Aaron and said, "I have sinned against the Lord your God and against you. Now forgive my sin once more and pray to the Lord your God to take this deadly plague away from me." Moses then left Pharaoh and prayed to the Lord. And the Lord changed the wind to a very strong west wind, which caught up the locusts and carried them into the Red Sea. Not a locust was left anywhere in Egypt. But the Lord hardened Pharaoh's heart, and he would not let the Israelites go. Then the Lord said to Moses, "Stretch out your hand toward the sky so that darkness spreads over Egypt—darkness that can be felt." So, Moses stretched out his hand toward the sky, and total darkness covered all Egypt for three days. No one could see anyone else or move about for three days. Yet all the Israelites had light in the places where they lived. Then Pharaoh summoned Moses and said, "Go, worship the Lord.

Even your women and children may go with you; only leave your flocks and herds behind." But Moses said, "You must allow us to have sacrifices and burnt offerings to present to the Lord our God. Our livestock too must go with us; not a hoof is to be left behind. We have to use some of them in worshiping the Lord our God, and until we get there, we will not know what we are to use to worship the Lord."

But the Lord hardened Pharaoh's heart, and he was not willing to let them go. Pharaoh said to Moses, "Get out of my sight! Make sure you do not appear before me again! The day you see my face you will die."

"Just as you say," Moses replied. "I will never appear before you again." Now the Lord had said to Moses, "I will bring one more plague on Pharaoh and on Egypt. After that, he will let you go from here, and when he does, he will drive you out completely. Tell the people that men and women alike are to ask their neighbors for articles of silver and gold." (The Lord made the Egyptians favorably disposed toward the people, and Moses himself was highly regarded in Egypt by Pharaoh's officials and by the people.) So, Moses said, "This is what the Lord says: 'About midnight I will go throughout Egypt. Every firstborn son in Egypt will die, from the firstborn son of Pharaoh, who sits on the throne, to the firstborn son of the female slave, who is at her hand mill, and all the firstborn of the cattle as well. There will be loud wailing throughout Egypt—worse than there has ever been or ever will be again. But among the Israelites not a dog will bark at any person or animal.' Then you will know that the Lord makes a distinction between Egypt and Israel. All these officials of yours will come to me, bowing down before me and saying, 'Go, you and all the people who follow you!' After that I will leave." Then Moses, hot with anger, left Pharaoh.

The Lord had said to Moses, "Pharaoh will refuse to listen to you—so that my wonders may be multiplied in Egypt." Moses and Aaron performed all these wonders before Pharaoh, but the Lord hardened Pharaoh's heart, and he would not let the Israelites go out of his country. [Exodus 7:1-22, 8:8-28, 9:10-35, 10 and 11 NIV]

The Stages of Purpose Fulfillment through Pharaoh: [Exodus 6, 7 NIV]

- *The Lord, God when He appeared to Abraham, Isaac and Jacob only revealed Himself to them as the Almighty, but was now going to reveal Himself to Israel through Pharaoh as the LORD [Exodus 6:3 NIV]. As the one in charge of everything, all things are by Him, for Him and through Him. He was about to display His sovereignty. Israel and Pharaoh were about to witness the unseen things before time began. I am the Lord, was about to perform by His mighty hand.*
- *The Hand of the Lord then began to perform His signs and wonders through the staff of the LORD in the hand of Moses and His words in the mouth of Aaron. Regardless of his resistance, God's power still prevailed over him. [Exodus 7:9-10 NIV]*

The Principles-

- *God is the LORD Almighty; all mighty is with and for God who is the LORD.*
  - *The hand of the Lord rules.*
  - *The hand of the Lord delivers.*
  - *The hand of the Lord establishes.*
  - *The hand of the Lord will never fail.*

The Object of Lesson: Israel.

Various men of the psalms summarized the life story and journey of Israel as psalms, their summary gives us the object of lessons from the life history of the people of Israel.

"As I meditate on all your works, I will consider your awesome deeds. God, your way is holy. What god is like our great God? God, you are the one performing awesome deeds. You reveal your might among the nations. You delivered[b] your people— the descendants of Jacob and Joseph— with your power. The waters saw you, God; the waters saw you and writhed. Indeed, the depths of the sea quaked. The clouds poured rain; the skies rumbled. Indeed, your lightning bolts flashed. Your thunderous sound was in a whirlwind; your lightning lights up the world; the earth becomes agitated and quakes. Your way was through the sea, and your path through mighty waters, but your footprints cannot be traced. You have led your people like a flock by the hands of Moses and Aaron." [Psalm 77:12-20 ISV]

"Listen, my people, to my instruction. Hear the words of my mouth.

I will tell a parable, speaking riddles from long ago- things that we have heard and known and that our ancestors related to us.

We will not withhold them from their descendants; we'll declare to the next generation the praises of the Lord-his might and awesome deeds that he has performed. He established a decree in Jacob, and established the Law in Israel, that he commanded our ancestors to reveal to their children in order that the next generation-children yet to be born- will know them and in turn teach them to their children.

Then they will put their trust in God and they will not forget his awesome deeds. Instead, they will keep his commandments.

They will not be like the rebellious generation of their ancestors, a rebellious generation, whose heart was not steadfast, and whose spirits were unfaithful to God. The Ephraimites were sharp shooters with the bow, but they retreated in the day of battle. They did not keep God's covenant, and refused to live by his Law. They have forgotten what he has done, his awesome deeds that they witnessed. He performed marvelous things in the presence of their ancestors in the land of Egypt-

in the fields of Zoan. He divided the sea so that they were able to cross; he caused the water to stand in a single location. He led them with a cloud during the day, and during the night with light from the fire.

He caused the rocks to split in the wilderness, and gave them water as from an abundant sea. He brought streams from rock, causing water to flow like a river. But time and again, they sinned against him, rebelling against the Most High in the desert. To test God was in their minds, when they demanded food to satisfy their cravings. They spoke against God by asking, "Is God able to prepare a feast in the desert?

It's true that Moses struck the rock so that water flowed forth and torrents of water gushed out, but is he also able to give bread or to supply meat for his people?" Therefore, when the Lord heard this, he was angry, and fire broke out against Jacob.

Moreover, his anger flared against Israel, because they didn't believe in God and didn't trust in his deliverance. Yet he commanded the skies above and the doors of the heavens to open, so that manna rained down on them for food and he sent them the grain of heaven.

Mortal men ate the food of angels; he sent provision to them in abundance. He stirred up the east wind in the heavens and drove the south wind by his might. He caused meat to rain on them like dust and winged birds as the sand of the sea. He caused these to fall in the middle of the camp and all around their tents. So, they ate and were very satisfied, because he granted their desire. However, before they had fulfilled their desire, while their food was still in their mouths, the anger of God flared against them, and he killed the strongest men and humbled Israel's young men. In spite of all of this, they kept on sinning and didn't believe in his marvelous deeds. So, he made their days end in futility, and their years with sudden terror. When he struck them, they sought him; they repented, and eagerly sought God.

Then they remembered that God was their rock, and the Most High God was their deliverer. But they deceived him with their mouths; they lied to him with their tongues. For their hearts weren't committed to him, and they weren't faithful to his covenant. But he, being merciful, forgave their iniquity and didn't destroy them; He restrained his anger and didn't vent all his wrath. For he remembered that they were only flesh, a passing wind that doesn't return. How they rebelled against him in the desert, grieving him in the wilderness! They tested God again and again, provoking the Holy One of Israel. They did not remember his power-the day he delivered them from their adversary, when he set his signs in Egypt and his wonders in the plain of Zoan.

He turned their rivers into blood and made their streams undrinkable.

He sent swarms of insects to bite them and frogs to destroy them.

He gave their crops to caterpillars and what they worked for to locusts.

He destroyed their vines with hail and their sycamore trees with frost.

He delivered their beasts to hail and their livestock to lightning bolts.

He inflicted his burning anger, wrath, indignation, and distress, sending destroying angels among them.

He blazed a path for his anger; he did not stop short from killing them, but handed them over to pestilence.

He struck every firstborn in Egypt, the first fruits of their manhood in the tents of Ham. Yet he led out his people like sheep, guiding them like a flock in the desert.

He led them to safety so they would not fear. As for their enemies, the sea covered them. He brought the people to the border of his holy mountain, which he acquired by his might. He drove out nations before them and allotted their tribal inheritance, settling the tribes of Israel in their tents. But they tested the Most High God by rebelling against him, and they did not obey his statutes. They fell away and were as disloyal as their ancestors. They became unreliable, like a defective bow; they angered him with their high places and with their carved images they made him jealous. God heard and became furious, and he completely rejected Israel.

He abandoned the tabernacle at Shiloh, the tent that he established among mankind. Then he sent his might into captivity and his glory into the control of the adversary. He delivered his people over to the sword and was angry with his possession. The young men were consumed by fire, and the virgins had no marriage celebrations. The priests fell by the sword, yet their widows couldn't weep. The Lord awoke as though from sleep, like a mighty warrior stimulated by wine. He beat back his adversaries, permanently disgracing them.

He rejected the clan of Joseph; and the tribe of Ephraim he did not choose. But he chose the tribe of Judah, the mountain of Zion, which he loves.

He built his sanctuary, high as the heavens, like the earth that he established forever. Then he chose his servant David, whom he took from the sheepfold. He brought him from birthing sheep to care for Jacob, his people, Israel, his possession. David shepherded them with a devoted heart, and led them with skillful hands." [Psalm 78:1-72 ISV]

"He remembers his eternal covenant – every promise he made for a thousand generations, like the covenant he made with Abraham, and his promise to Isaac. He presented it to Jacob as a decree, to Israel as an everlasting covenant. He said: "I will give Canaan to you as the allotted portion that is your inheritance." When the Hebrews were few in number-so very few-and were sojourners in it, they wandered from nation to nation, from one kingdom to another. He did not allow anyone to oppress them, or any kings to reprove them. "Don't touch my anointed or hurt my prophets!" He declared a famine on the land; destroying the entire food supply. He sent a man before them- Joseph, who had been sold as a slave. They bound his feet with fetters and placed an iron collar on his neck, until the time his prediction came true, as the word of the Lord refined him. He sent a king who released him, a ruler of people who set him free. He made him the master over his household, the manager of all his possessions- to discipline his rulers at will and make his elders wise. Then Israel came to Egypt; indeed, Jacob lived in the land of Ham. He caused his people to multiply greatly; and be more numerous than their enemies. He caused them to hate his people and to deceive his servants...... Indeed, he remembered his sacred promise to his servant Abraham. He led his people out with gladness, his chosen ones with shouts of joy. He gave to them the land of nations; they inherited the labor of other people so they might keep his statutes and observe his laws." [Psalm 105:8-25, 42-45 ISV]

"In Egypt, our ancestors neither comprehended your awesome deeds nor remembered your abundant gracious love. Instead, they rebelled beside the sea, the Reed Sea. He delivered for the sake of his name, to make his power known. He shouted at the Reed Sea and it dried up; and led them through the sea as though through a desert. He delivered them from the power of their foe; redeeming them from the power of their enemy. The water overwhelmed their enemies, so that not one of them survived. Then they believed his word and sung his praise. But they quickly forgot his deeds and did not wait for his counsel. They were overwhelmed with craving in the wilderness, so God tested them in the wasteland. God granted them their request, but sent leanness into their lives. They were envious of Moses in the camp,

and of Aaron, the holy one of the Lord. The earth opened and swallowed Dathan, closing over Abiram's clan. Then a fire burned among their company, a flame that set the wicked ablaze. They fashioned a calf at Horeb and worshipped a carved image. They exchanged their glory with the image of a grass-eating bull. They forgot God their Savior, who performed great things in Egypt-awesome deeds in the land of Ham, astonishing deeds at the Reed Sea. He would have destroyed them but for Moses, his chosen one, who stood in the breach before him to avert his destructive wrath. They rejected the desirable land, and they didn't trust his promise. They murmured in their tents, and didn't listen to the voice of the Lord. So, he swore an oath concerning them-that he would cause them to die in the wilderness, to cause their children to perish among the nations and be scattered among many lands. For they adopted the worship of Baal Peor and ate sacrifices offered to the dead. They had provoked anger by their deeds, so that a plague broke out against them. But Phinehas intervened and prayed so that the plague was restrained. And it was credited to him as a righteous act, from generation to generation-to eternity. They provoked wrath at the waters of Meribah, and Moses suffered on account of them. For they rebelled against him, so that he spoke thoughtlessly with his lips. They never destroy the people, as the Lord had commanded them. Instead, they mingled among the nations and learned their ways. They worshipped their idols, and this became a trap for them. They sacrificed their sons and daughters to demons. They shed innocent blood- the blood of their sons and daughters- whom they sacrificed to the idols of Canaan, thereby polluting the land with blood.

Therefore, they became unclean because of what they did; they have acted like whores by their evil deeds. The Lord's anger burned against his people, so that he despised his own inheritance. He turned them over to domination by nations where those who hated them ruled over them. Their enemies oppressed them, so that they were humiliated by their power. He delivered them many times, but they demonstrated rebellion by their evil plans; therefore, they sunk deep in their sins. Yet when he saw their distress and heard their cries for help, he remembered his covenant with them, and so relented according to the greatness of his gracious love. He caused all their captors to show compassion toward them. [Psalm 106:7-46 ISV]

"He sent his servant Moses, along with Aaron, whom he had chosen. He performed His signs among them, His wonders in the land of Ham. He sent darkness, and it became dark. He turned their water into blood, so that the fish died. Their land swarmed with frogs even to the chambers of their kings. He spoke, and a swarm of insects invaded their land. He set hail instead of rain, and lightning throughout their land. It destroyed their vines and their figs, breaking trees throughout their country. Then He commanded the locust to come-grasshoppers without number. They consumed every green plant in their land, and devoured the fruit of their soil. He struck down every firstborn in their land, the first fruits of all their progeny. Then He brought Israel out with silver and gold, and no one among His tribes stumbled. The Egyptians rejoiced when they left, because fear of Israel descended on them. He spread out a cloud for a cover, and fire for light at night. Israel asked, and quail came; food from heaven satisfied them. He opened a rock, and water gushed out flowing like a river in the desert" [Psalm 108:26-41 ISV]

"When Israel came out of Egypt-the household of Jacob from a people of foreign speech- Judah became God's sanctuary, Israel his place of dominion. The sea saw this and fled, the Jordan River ran backwards, the mountains skipped like rams, and the hills like lambs. What happened to you, sea, that you fled? Jordan, that you ran backwards? Mountains that you skipped like rams? And you hill, that you skipped like lambs? Tremble then, earth, at the presence of the Lord, at the presence of the God of Jacob, who turned the rock into a pool of water, the flinty rock into flowing springs." [Psalm 114:1-8 ISV]

In the Promise Land through In the Wilderness.

Before the Hebrews would enter the land of promise, they had to pass through the wilderness, in the wilderness they had various encounters and experiences that shaped the cause and destiny of them all.

The Stages of Purpose Fulfillment through Wilderness:

- *The Passover: The Passover was the transportation from one dominion – Egypt to another dominion – God's power. It was their transfer from one state of being to another, death to life, bondage to freedom. All this was made possible by the power of the blood of the sacrificed lamb which became their meal of strength, The Passover meal. [Exodus 12:1-28 ISV]*
- *The Reed Sea Crossover: After every Passover is the cross over, the cross over is the passing through of the reed sea, it is the washing by the flowing water, to cleanse and purify by immersion. [Exodus 14:21-22 ISV]*
- *The Pillar of Cloud and Fire: The cloud covers and the fire lights path to guide, the fire heats to provide weather regulation and protection in a wilderness. All the people went through the blood of the lamb, the water of the sea, and they all went under the pillar of cloud and fire by the hand of Moses, this was the people's immersion into Moses through the blood, the sea, the cloud and fire. This going through and immersion is, immersion into Christ Jesus' blood by the Passover, the Spirit's regeneration and renewal by the washing of the Cross Over and the Spirit's leading by the pillar of cloud and fire. [Exodus 13:21 ISV]*
- *The Manna – The Rock Water: The manna was the spiritual food and the water from the rock was the spiritual water from the spiritual rock for them to eat and drink for sustenance. All the people ate the same spiritual food and drank the same spiritual drink, as they drank from the spiritual rock that went with them. That spiritual food and spiritual rock was the Christ and the Spirit of Christ. [Exodus 13:15, 17:6, 1 Corinthians 10:1-4 NIV]*
- *The Tabernacle of the covenant of law: Now in the wilderness, the Most High patterned what was in heaven on earth – the tabernacle or tent of meeting, so His presence could dwell with His people. The Ark of the Covenant, the laws of the covenant were placed in the tabernacle of the LORD to foreshadow what was to come in the Messiah. [Exodus 26:1 NIV]*

Questions and Lessons from Israel:

The life of the people of ancient Israel teaches us many lessons in our modern age, and it gives us many questions also to ask and answer. Why was God performing all this signs and wonders for a particular group of people in all of the earth? Some questions we can ask and learn lessons from are that, can there be a people of God;

- *Who will not comprehend the deeds of God?*
- *Who forget God's gracious love?*
- *Who forget God's deeds?*
- *Who rebel against God; not waiting for His counsel and plan to unfold?*
- *Who become self-craving and God testing, seeking after their own selfish desires with covetousness and putting the might and Holiness of the Most High to test? Doubting His power to perform.*
- *Who envy God's leaders in position?*
- *Who exchange God's glory for other self-made images; idolatry?*
- *Who reject and despise the desirable pleasant land, the Lord's promised land of rest?*
- *Who will not trust or believe in God's promise?*
- *Who grumble and murmur?*
- *Who adopt false worship?*

In all of these;

- *We must Comprehend God and His deeds.*
- *We must not Compromise our position in His promise.*
- *We must not Complain when faced with difficulty in the wilderness.*
- *We must not Conform to the standard of the "world".*
- *We must not be Contumacious.*
- *We must not rebel against and reject the Spirit of God, and revel in our cravings.*
- *We must be steadfast in heart toward God and His promise.*
- *We must be faithful in spirit toward God.*
- *We must be righteous with God.*

The Man After God's Heart, David.

Later in time, God will raise a shepherd to lead His people and nation as king, his life was later to be a model for the ultimate plans and purposes of God and the restoration of all humanity.

The Shepherd King:

"The Lord said to Samuel, "How long will you mourn for Saul, since I have rejected him as king over Israel? Fill your horn with oil and be on your way; I am sending you to Jesse of Bethlehem. I have chosen one of his sons to be king." But Samuel said, "How can I go? If Saul hears about it, he will kill me." The Lord said, "Take a heifer with you and say, 'I have come to sacrifice to the Lord.' Invite Jesse to the sacrifice, and I will show you what to do. You are to anoint for me the one I indicate." Samuel did what the Lord said. When he arrived at Bethlehem, the elders of the town trembled when they met him. They asked, "Do you come in peace?" Samuel replied, "Yes, in peace; I have come to sacrifice to the Lord. Consecrate yourselves and come to the sacrifice with me." Then he consecrated Jesse and his sons and invited them to the sacrifice. When they arrived, Samuel saw Eliab and thought, "Surely the Lord's anointed stands here before the Lord." But the Lord said to Samuel, "Do not consider his appearance or his height, for I have rejected him. The Lord does not look at the things people look at. People look at the outward appearance, but the Lord looks at the heart." Then Jesse called Abinadab and had him pass in front of Samuel. But Samuel said, "The Lord has not chosen this one either." Jesse then had Shammah pass by, but Samuel said, "Nor has the Lord chosen this one." Jesse had seven of his sons pass before Samuel, but Samuel said to him, "The Lord has not chosen these." So, he asked Jesse, "Are these all the sons you have?" "There is still the youngest," Jesse answered. "He is tending the sheep." Samuel said, "Send for him; we will not sit down until he arrives."

So, he sent for him and had him brought in. He was glowing with health and had a fine appearance and handsome features. Then the Lord said, "Rise and anoint him; this is the one." So, Samuel took the horn of oil and anointed him in the presence of his brothers, and from that day on the Spirit of the Lord came powerfully upon David. Samuel then went to Ramah." [1 Samuel 16:1-13 NIV]

The young shepherd boy who was the son of the Ephrathite of Bethlehem in Judah was anointed king but before he would ascend to the throne, the Lord will train and prepare him through a series of events to reveal and refine his heart. It is in these experiences of his life that it shows that he was a man after the Lord's own heart rather than just the prestige, position, power, prominence or pride of being the anointed one.

The young anointed king needed to gain experience in handling the kingship affairs, so the Lord provided the opportunity for him to meet the then present king, Saul. The means by which he would meet him was that, war was raging between the people of Israel and the Philistine, he as a young boy was not permitted to enlist in the war but was the keeper of sheep in the wilderness, one day, he was sent by the father to deliver food supply to his brother, upon his arrival, he questioned some members of the army about the reward which would go to the man who conquers the champion of the Philistine who had been tormenting the Israelites for forty days and nights. These elder brothers when they overheard his conversations were angered by him, so he said,

"Now what have I done?" said David. "Can't I even speak?" He then turned away to someone else and brought up the same matter, and the men answered him as before." [1 Samuel 17:29-30 NIV]

David's words were overheard and reported to king Saul such that the king sent for him to be brought to him. When he came to the king he said, *"Let no one lose heart on account of this Philistine; your servant will go and fight him."* [1 Samuel 17:32 NIV]

Saul discouraged him saying, *"You are not able to go out against this Philistine and fight him; you are only a young man, and he has been a warrior from his youth."* [1 Samuel 17:33 NIV]

Yet David would not be discouraged by this experience king warrior, so he told Saul of his experience with the life of a shepherd living in the wilderness with the wild voracious animals and his confidence in the Lord, *"Your servant has been keeping his father's sheep. When a lion or a bear came and carried off a sheep from the flock, I went after it, struck it and rescued the sheep from its mouth. When it turned on me, I seized it by its hair, struck it and killed it. Your servant has killed both the lion and the bear; this uncircumcised Philistine will be like one of them, because he has defied the armies of the living God. The Lord who rescued me from the paw of the lion and the paw of the bear will rescue me from the hand of this Philistine."* [1 Samuel 17:34-37 NIV]

Saul now, then turned to hesitantly encourage David by saying to him, *"Go, and the Lord be with you."* [1 Samuel 17:37 NIV]

But he then sought to equip the young warrior with his old tools for warfare, *"Saul dressed David in his own tunic. He put a coat of armor on him and a bronze helmet on his head."* [1 Samuel 17:38 NIV]

This armory was unusual to this sling and stones warrior, his armory of expertise are slings and stones, not tunic, coat of armor or bronze helmet which he had not tried nor tested before, so he said, *"I cannot go in these, because I am not used to them. So, he took them off."* [1 Samuel 17:39 NIV]

David then turned to his own tried and tested weapons of war of staff in his hand, and choosing five smooth stones from the stream, he put them into the pouch of his shepherd's bag, whiles his sling was in his hand, he went ahead to approach the Philistine who was by then dressed as a mighty warrior, with his shield bearer in front of him, his Philistine companion when he approached David looked and saw that he was little more than a boy, glowing with health and handsome, so he despised him by saying, *"Am I a dog, that you come at me with sticks?"* he cursed David by his gods. *"Come here,"* he said, *"and I'll give your flesh to the birds and the wild animals!"* [1 Samuel 17:43-44 NIV]

David, unafraid and not timid, responded not in his own strength but that of the Lord to the Philistine, *"You come against me with sword and spear and javelin, but I come against you in the name of the Lord Almighty, the God of the armies of Israel, whom you have defied. This day the Lord will deliver you into my hands, and I'll strike you down and cut off your head. This very day I will give the carcasses of the Philistine army to the birds and the wild animals, and the whole world will know that there is a God in Israel. All those gathered here will know that it is not by sword or spear that the Lord saves; for the battle is the Lord's, and he will give all of you into our hands." As the Philistine moved closer to attack him, David ran quickly toward the battle line to meet him. Reaching into his bag and taking out a stone, he slung it and struck the Philistine on the forehead. The stone sank into his forehead, and he fell face down on the ground.*

So, David triumphed over the Philistine with a sling and a stone; without a sword in his hand he struck down the Philistine and killed him. David ran and stood over him. He took hold of the Philistine's sword and drew it from the sheath. After he killed him, he cut off his head with the sword.

When the Philistines saw that their hero was dead, they turned and ran. Then the men of Israel and Judah surged forward with a shout and pursued the Philistines to the entrance of Gath and to the gates of Ekron. Their dead were strewn along the Shaaraim road to Gath and Ekron. When the Israelites returned from chasing the Philistines, they plundered their camp. David took the Philistine's head and brought it to Jerusalem; he put the Philistine's weapons in his own tent. As Saul watched David going out to meet the Philistine, he said to Abner, commander of the army, "Abner, whose son is that young man?" Abner replied, "As surely as you live, Your Majesty, I don't know." The king said, "Find out whose son this young man is." As soon as David returned from killing the Philistine, Abner took him and brought him before Saul, with David still holding the Philistine's head. "Whose son are you, young man?" Saul asked him. David said, "I am the son of your servant Jesse of Bethlehem." [1 Samuel 17:45-58 NIV]

The battle was the Lord's, and indeed He granted the victory to His young anointed king so that he would gain access into the palace for him to be trained in kingship, moving him from tending sheep to tending His people.

The Stages of Purpose Fulfillment for David: [1 Samuel 16,17 NIV]

- *In the house of Jesse, David was found and chosen, the youngest son who was not counted, made an outcast, rejected and abounded by family but accepted by God. [1 Samuel 16:12 NIV]*
- *In the battle field, faced with numerous challenges and battles, he overcame them all with the strength of God, from lions to bears, to Goliath to Armies. [1 Samuel 17:34-37, 50 NIV]*
- *In the house of Saul, he is to learn firsthand from the king yet he becomes an enemy to the king.*
- *In the wilderness, he is sent to the wilderness of life to learn the lessons of dependence and obedience on the sovereign one.*
- *In the palace, in and through all of these, he returns to the palace as the king of the Lord to build the kingdom of Israel as the Lord desired.*

The Oath:

The Creator of the heavens and earth made a covenant with a young shepherd boy, and He took an oath which He was not going to violate. His oath served as the legitimacy for the kingship of David, and it also deepened his relationship with the Creator. Regardless of the enemies he was going to face, the Creator was going to establish him, He was going to be his rock, fortress, refuge, strength and shield. This was a covenant based on the sovereignty of the Creator, because He had found and chosen a man after His own heart. This shepherd boy only wanted to know the heart of God, so God also greatly loved him. He was the man of His choosing! Through him the Creator was now going to establish His kingdom over His people. He was going to build a city for him.

"You said, "I have made a covenant with my chosen one, I have sworn to David my servant, 'I will establish your line forever and make your throne firm through all generations.'" Once you spoke in a vision, to your faithful people you said: "I have bestowed strength on a warrior; I have raised up a young man from among the people. I have found David my servant; with my sacred oil I have anointed him. My hand will sustain him; surely my arm will strengthen him. The enemy will not get the better of him; the wicked will not oppress him. I will crush his foes before him and strike down his adversaries. My faithful love will be with him, and through my name his horn will be exalted. I will set his hand over the sea, his right hand over the rivers. He will call out to me, 'You are my Father, my God, the Rock my Savior.' And I will appoint him to be my firstborn, the most exalted of the kings of the earth. I will maintain my love to him forever, and my covenant with him will never fail. I will establish his line forever, his throne as long as the heavens endure. "If his sons forsake my law and do not follow my statutes, if they violate my decrees and fail to keep my commands, I will punish their sin with the rod, their iniquity with flogging; but I will not take my love from him, nor will I ever betray my faithfulness. I will not violate my covenant or alter what my lips have uttered. Once for all, I have sworn by my holiness— and I will not lie to David— that his line will continue forever and his throne endure before me like the sun; it will be established forever like the moon, the faithful witness in the sky."" [Psalm 89:3-4, 19-37 NIV]

"The Lord made an oath to David from which he will not retreat [revoke]: "One of your sons I will set in place on your throne. For the Lord has chosen Zion, desiring it as his dwelling place. "This is my resting place forever. Here I will live, because I desire to do so. I will bless its provisions abundantly; I will satiate its poor with bread. I will clothe its priests with salvation and its godly ones will shout for joy. There I will create a power base for David- I have prepared a lamp for my anointed one. I will clothe his enemies with disgrace, but on him his crown will shine." [Psalm 132:11-18 ISV]

The Promises of God to David; [Psalm 89:27-29, 132-11-18 NIV]

- *The king, would be appointed as the "firstborn" of the Lord. [Psalm 89:27 NIV]*
- *The king, would be the most exalted king of kings of the earth, to rule from river to river and sea to sea. [Psalm 89:27 NIV]*
- *The "son of David" would be placed on the throne forever. [Psalm 132:11ISV]*
- *The son, would call out to the Lord, as my Father, my God, the Rock my Savior. [Psalm 89:26 NIV]*

- *The line of David would be established forever as long as the heavens endure and his throne be firm through all generations. [Psalm 89:29 NIV]*
- *The resting place of God forever is Zion because He God desired and chose it. [Psalm 132:14 ISV]*
- *The priests of Zion would be clothed with salvation. [Psalm 132:16 ISV]*
- *The godly in Zion would rejoice. [Psalm 132:16 ISV]*
- *The blessing of abundant provision would be in Zion. [Psalm 132:15 ISV]*
- *The poor in Zion would be satiated with bread. [Psalm 132:15 ISV]*
- *The power base for David would be created in Zion. [Psalm 132:17 ISV]*
- *The lamp would be prepared for the anointed one. [Psalm 132:17 ISV]*
- *The enemies of the anointed one would be clothed with disgrace. [Psalm 132:18 ISV]*
- *God would maintain His faithfulness, love, mercy, justice, righteousness, grace, HIMSELF to him forever, and His covenant with him would never fail. [Psalm 89:28 NIV]*

The Principles-

God wanted the oath He was taking with David to be secured, therefore, He based the covenant on Himself, He swore by His, faithfulness as the creator of the universe, telling Him that as the created universe exist by the ruling and function of Himself, so also, the covenant was going to exist and function even till its fulfillment. As the faithful one, He was not going to violate His covenant with His servant David.

Again, the basis of the covenant was the love of God, since God Himself is love, He was going to love David and the covenant He had made with and for him. He was not going to retreat from His love for him by the covenant neither was He going to revoke the covenant of love by any actions of the descents of David.

Furthermore, the mercies and graciousness of the eternal one would be with him forever and ever, nothing and no one was going to change or revoke this covenant. [Psalm 89:3-4, 19-37 ISV]

Next of kin in line.

Every king needs an heir, every success needs a successor, and for succession to continue there was a need for the successor to the throne of David. David, after he received the oath and promise of God to have a kingdom that last forever, with his seed to be the heir to his throne, made a prayer for the king's son, the son of David who would inherit the throne and the kingdom. David was by the Spirit, interceding for the future king, this was because he had an understanding of the covenant the Lord had made with him, it has been called; *"Davidic Prayer for the King, for the Solomonic Kingdom."*

"God, endow the king with ability to render your justice, and the king's son to render your right

decisions. *May he rule your people with right decisions and your oppressed ones with justice. May the mountains bring prosperity to the people and the hills bring righteousness. May he defend the afflicted of the people and deliver the children of the poor, but crush the oppressor. May they fear you as long as the sun and moon shine-from generation to generation. May he be like the rain that descends on mown grass, like showers sprinkling on the ground. The righteous will flourish at the proper time and peace will prevail until the moon is no more. May he rule from sea to sea, from the Euphrates River to the ends of the earth. May the nomads bow down before him, and his enemies lick the dust. May the kings of Tarshish and of distant shores bring gifts, and may the kings of Sheba and Seba offer tribute.*

May all kings bow down to him, and all nations serve him. For he will deliver the needy when they cry out for help, and the poor when there is no deliverer. He will have compassion on the poor and the needy, and he will save the lives of the needy. He will redeem them from oppression and violence, since their lives are precious in his sight.

May he live long and be given gold from Sheba, and may prayer be offered for him continually, and may he be blessed every day.

May grain be abundant in the land all the way to the mountain tops;

may its fruits flourish like the forests of Lebanon, and may the cities sprout like the grass of the earth. May his fame be eternal-as long as the sun may his name endure and may they be blessed through him and may all nations call him blessed. Blessed be the Lord God, the God of Israel, who alone does awesome deeds. And blessed be his glorious name forever, and may the whole earth be filled with his glory. Amen and amen! This ends the prayers of Jesse's son David." [Psalm 72:1-20 ISV]

This was a king's prayer to the future king, the king's son and the king's kingdom. This prayer was ultimately fulfilled in the life of the Messiah Jesus not just Solomon even though it was same during the reign of Solomon. Let us look at key figures of this prayer.

- *The king, endowed with ability by God was to render God's justice, and to render God's right decisions.* [Psalm 72:1 ISV]
- *The king was to rule God's people with right decisions and God's oppressed ones with justice.* [Psalm 72:2 ISV]
- *The king was to be the defender of the afflicted of the people.* [Psalm 72:4 ISV]
- *The king was to be the deliverer of the children of the poor, but the crusher of the oppressor.* [Psalm 72:4 ISV]
  'For he will deliver the needy when they cry out for help, and the poor when there is no deliverer. He will have compassion on the poor and the needy, and he will save the lives of the needy. He will redeem them from oppression and violence, since their lives are precious in his sight.' [Psalm 72:12-14 ISV]
- *The king was to fear God as long as the sun and moon shine-from generation to generation.* [Psalm 72:5 ISV]

- *The kingdom was to be like the rain that descends on mown grass, like showers sprinkling on the ground. [Psalm 72:6 ISV]*
- *The king was to live long and prayer was to be offered for him continually, and he was to be blessed every day. [Psalm 72:15 ISV]*
- *The king's fame was to be eternal - as long as the sun and his name was to endure. [Psalm 72:17 ISV]*
- *The king was to be the blessings to all nations, through him all nations were to be blessed and all nations were to call him blessed. [Psalm 72:17 ISV]*
- *The mountains were to bring prosperity to the people that the king ruled over and the hills bring righteousness. Grain was to be abundant in the land all the way to the mountain tops; the kingdoms lands' fruits were to flourish like the forests of Lebanon, and the cities of the kingdom were to sprout like the grass of the earth. [Psalm 72:16 ISV]*
- *At the time of the king, the righteous would flourish at the proper time and peace will prevail until the moon is no more. [Psalm 72:7 ISV]*
- *The king was to rule from sea to sea, from the Euphrates River to the ends of the earth. [Psalm 72:8 ISV]*
- *The nomads were to bow down before the king, and the king's enemies were to lick the dust. [Psalm 72:9 ISV]*
- *The kings of Tarshish and of distant shores were to bring gifts, and the kings of Sheba and Seban were to offer tribute to the king; he was to be given gold from Sheba. [Psalm 72:10 ISV]*
- *All kings were to bow down to him, and all nations were to serve him. [Psalm 72:11 ISV]*

CHAPTER FOUR

The Law and the Prophets.

The prophets of old all searched, investigated intently and with greatest of care the era of time the Spirit of God was telling them of the appearance of Jesus as the Christ and salvation. His birth was foretold, His life, death and rise from the death were all predicted before its time of fulfillment. The prophets and the people were anticipating this coming king and kingdom that was so promising and beautiful. The writings of the prophets and the law gives descriptions of the picture of His king and His kingdom, they portrayed pictures of the king's kingdom. Let's look at some words of the future that were shown to Isaiah about the counsel of God concerning the age that was coming.

- ***Isaiah:***
   "Isaiah said, "Hear now, you house of David! Is it not enough to try the patience of humans? Will you try the patience of my God also? Therefore, the Lord himself will give you a sign: The virgin will conceive and give birth to a son, and will call him Immanuel." [Isaiah 7:13-14 NIV]
   "Nevertheless, there will be no more gloom for those who were in distress. In the past he humbled the land of Zebulun and the land of Naphtali, but in the future he will honor Galilee of the nations, by the Way of the Sea, beyond the Jordan—The people walking in darkness have seen a great light; on those living in the land of deep darkness a light has dawned. You have enlarged the nation and increased their joy; they rejoice before you as people rejoice at the harvest, as warriors rejoice when dividing the plunder. For as in the day of Midian's defeat, you have shattered the yoke that burdens them, the bar across their shoulders, the rod of their oppressor. Every warrior's boot used in battle and every garment rolled in blood will be destined for burning, will be fuel for the fire. For to us a child is born, to us a son is given, and the government will be on his shoulders. And he will be called Wonderful Counselor, Mighty God, Everlasting Father, Prince of Peace. Of the greatness of his government and peace there will be no end. He will reign on David's throne and over his kingdom, establishing and upholding it with justice and righteousness from that time on and forever. The zeal of the Lord Almighty will accomplish this." [Isaiah 9:1-7 NIV]

"A shoot will come up from the stump of Jesse; from his roots a Branch will bear fruit. The Spirit of the Lord will rest on him—the Spirit of wisdom and of understanding, the Spirit of counsel and of might, the Spirit of the knowledge and fear of the Lord—and he will delight in the fear of the Lord. He will not judge by what he sees with his eyes, or decide by what he hears with his ears; but with righteousness he will judge the needy, with justice he will give decisions for the poor of the earth. He will strike the earth with the rod of his mouth; with the breath of his lips he will slay the wicked. Righteousness will be his belt and faithfulness the sash around his waist. The wolf will live with the lamb, the leopard will lie down with the goat, the calf and the lion and the yearling together; and a little child will lead them. The cow will feed with the bear, their young will lie down together, and the lion will eat straw like the ox. The infant will play near the cobra's den, and the young child will put its hand into the viper's nest. They will neither harm nor destroy on all my holy mountain, for the earth will be filled with the knowledge of the Lord as the waters cover the sea. In that day the Root of Jesse will stand as a banner for the peoples; the nations will rally to him, and his resting place will be glorious." [Isaiah 11:1-10 NIV]

""Here is my servant, whom I uphold, my chosen one in whom I delight; I will put my Spirit on him, and he will bring justice to the nations. He will not shout or cry out, or raise his voice in the streets.

A bruised reed he will not break, and a smoldering wick he will not snuff out. In faithfulness he will bring forth justice; he will not falter or be discouraged till he establishes justice on earth. In his teaching the islands will put their hope." This is what God the Lord says— the Creator of the heavens, who stretches them out, who spreads out the earth with all that springs from it, who gives breath to its people, and life to those who walk on it: "I, the Lord, have called you in righteousness; I will take hold of your hand. I will keep you and will make you to be a covenant for the people and a light for the Gentiles, to open eyes that are blind, to free captives from prison and to release from the dungeon those who sit in darkness. "I am the Lord; that is my name! I will not yield my glory to another or my praise to idols. See, the former things have taken place, and new things I declare; before they spring into being, I announce them to you."" [Isaiah 42:1-9 NIV].

"See, my servant will act wisely; he will be raised and lifted up and highly exalted. Just as there were many who were appalled at him—his appearance was so disfigured beyond that of any human being and his form marred beyond human likeness— so he will sprinkle many nations, and kings will shut their mouths because of him. For what they were not told, they will see, and what they have not heard, they will understand." [Isaiah 52:13-15 NIV]

"Who has believed our message and to whom has the arm of the Lord been revealed? He grew up before him like a tender shoot, and like a root out of dry ground. He had no beauty or majesty to attract us to him, nothing in his appearance that we should desire him. He was despised and rejected by mankind, a man of suffering, and familiar with pain.

Like one from whom people hide their faces he was despised, and we held him in low esteem. Surely he took up our pain and bore our suffering, yet we considered him punished by God, stricken by him, and afflicted. But he was pierced for our transgressions, he was crushed for our iniquities; the punishment that brought us peace was on him, and by his wounds we are healed. We all, like sheep, have gone astray, each of us has turned to our own way; and the Lord has laid on him the iniquity of us all. He was oppressed and afflicted, yet he did not open his mouth; he was led like a lamb to the slaughter, and as a sheep before its shearers is silent, so he did not open his mouth. By oppression and judgment he was taken away. Yet who of his generation protested? For he was cut off from the land of the living; for the transgression of my people he was punished. He was assigned a grave with the wicked, and with the rich in his death, though he had done no violence, nor was any deceit in his mouth. Yet it was the Lord's will to crush him and cause him to suffer, and though the Lord makes his life an offering for sin, he will see his offspring and prolong his days, and the will of the Lord will prosper in his hand. After he has suffered, he will see the light of life and be satisfied; by his knowledge my righteous servant will justify many, and he will bear their iniquities. Therefore I will give him a portion among the great, and he will divide the spoils with the strong, because he poured out his life unto death, and was numbered with the transgressors. For he bore the sin of many, and made intercession for the transgressors." [Isaiah 53:1-12 NIV]

""Arise, shine, for your light has come, and the glory of the Lord rises upon you. See, darkness covers the earth and thick darkness is over the peoples, but the Lord rises upon you and his glory appears over you.

Nations will come to your light, and kings to the brightness of your dawn. "Lift up your eyes and look about you: All assemble and come to you; your sons come from afar, and your daughters are carried on the hip. Then you will look and be radiant, your heart will throb and swell with joy; the wealth on the seas will be brought to you, to you the riches of the nations will come. Herds of camels will cover your land, young camels of Midian and Ephah. And all from Sheba will come, bearing gold and incense and proclaiming the praise of the Lord." [Isaiah 60:1-6 NIV]

"The Spirit of the Sovereign Lord is on me, because the Lord has anointed me to proclaim good news to the poor. He has sent me to bind up the brokenhearted, to proclaim freedom for the captives and release from darkness for the prisoners, to proclaim the year of the Lord's favor and the day of vengeance of our God, to comfort all who mourn, and provide for those who grieve in Zion—to bestow on them a crown of beauty instead of ashes, the oil of joy instead of mourning, and a garment of praise instead of a spirit of despair. They will be called oaks of righteousness, a planting of the Lord for the display of his splendor.

They will rebuild the ancient ruins and restore the places long devastated; they will renew the ruined cities that have been devastated for generations. Strangers will shepherd your flocks; foreigners will work your fields and vineyards. And you will be called priests of the Lord, you will be named ministers of our God. You will feed on the wealth of nations, and in their riches you will boast. Instead of your shame you will receive a double portion, and instead of disgrace you will rejoice in your inheritance. And so, you will inherit a double portion in your land, and everlasting joy will be yours. "For I, the Lord, love justice; I hate robbery and wrongdoing. In my faithfulness I will reward my people and make an everlasting covenant with them. Their descendants will be known among the nations and their offspring among the peoples. All who see them will acknowledge that they are a people the Lord has blessed." I delight greatly in the Lord; my soul rejoices in my God. For he has clothed me with garments of salvation and arrayed me in a robe of his righteousness, as a bridegroom adorns his head like a priest, and as a bride adorns herself with her jewels. For as the soil makes the sprout come up and a garden causes seeds to grow, so the Sovereign Lord will make righteousness and praise spring up before all nations." [Isaiah 61:1-11 NIV]

From the inspired words of counsel revealed to Isaiah, we see various intents of God. Some of which are;

- *A virgin was going to conceive and give birth to a son called Immanuel, meaning God in man and God with man, which was to be as a sign of God's power at work in man because His patience was being tried by the House of David. [Isaiah 7:13-14 NIV]*
- *A great light was to dawn. The great light which was dawning was going to cause people living in darkness to see light. Those people living in distress would no longer see gloom and they would rejoice with the sounds of victory and enlargement from the triumph of this great light in battle. [Isaiah 9:1-3 NIV]*
- *A child was to be born and a son was to be given. The born child and given son was bringing the government as his assignment with his name being Wonderful Counselor, Mighty God, Everlasting Father, and Prince of Peace. His government would be one of greatness with peace where there will be no end. His throne of rulership and reign would be that of David's kingdom, he would establish and uphold his kingdom government with justice and righteousness from that time that he would be born and forever. [Isaiah 9:6-7 NIV]*
- *A warrior who was going to deliver from the hands of the oppressor. [Isaiah 9:4 NIV]*
- *A shoot was to come out from the stump of Jesse (father of David), his root would bear fruit with the Spirit of the Lord that rests on him. The Spirit of the Lord on him would be the Spirit of wisdom, understanding, counsel, might, knowledge and reverential fear for the Lord, so that he can be a just judge with righteousness and faithfulness. His resting place of judgment was to be glorious and a banner to all people rallying to him. [Isaiah 11:1-3, 11:10NIV]*
- *A chosen servant by the Lord with His Spirit was to bring justice to the nations. He will faithfully establish and bring forth justice to all the earth. He was not going to falter, fail or be discouraged and by his teaching, he would bring hope, light, freedom, and deliverance to all. [Isaiah 42:1-4 NIV]*
- *A wise servant was going to act wisely, be highly lifted up and exalted, to be disfigured in his physical appearance, marred beyond any human likeness and also appealed by men by this His blood would sprinkle many nations, and kings will shut their mouths because of him. He would suffer injustice, oppression, wickedness and death for the sake of humanity. [Isaiah 52:13-15 NIV]*
- *And finally, the light came, so Isaiah announced that the people arise, and shine for their light, the promised one had come and the glory of the Lord was risen on them. [Isaiah 60:1 NIV] The*

Spirit of the Sovereign Lord was his light and the Spirit gave him anointing to proclaim the good news of all that he was coming to do to all people; the poor, brokenhearted, captive, prisoners, mourners, and grievers. He was establishing his kingdom government to serve the people with the light of justice, righteousness, peace, freedom, beauty, oil of joy, garment of praise, double portion of blessing, wealth and inheritance so that they will be oaks of righteousness planted by the Lord, priest of the Lord, ministers of God to display his splendor. [Isaiah 9:2-5, 7 ISV]

- *The zeal of the Lord Almighty would be the hand and the heart to accomplish all that was being revealed to the people through the prophet. [Isaiah 9:7 NIV]*

- ### *Daniel*:

"In the second year of his reign, Nebuchadnezzar had dreams; his mind was troubled and he could not sleep. So, the king summoned the magicians, enchanters, sorcerers and astrologers to tell him what he had dreamed. When they came in and stood before the king, he said to them, "I have had a dream that troubles me and I want to know what it means." Then the astrologers answered the king, "May the king live forever! Tell your servants the dream, and we will interpret it." The king replied to the astrologers, "This is what I have firmly decided: If you do not tell me what my dream was and interpret it, I will have you cut into pieces and your houses turned into piles of rubble. But if you tell me the dream and explain it, you will receive from me gifts and rewards and great honor. So, tell me the dream and interpret it for me."

Once more they replied, "Let the king tell his servants the dream, and we will interpret it." Then the king answered, "I am certain that you are trying to gain time, because you realize that this is what I have firmly decided: If you do not tell me the dream, there is only one penalty for you. You have conspired to tell me misleading and wicked things, hoping the situation will change. So then, tell me the dream, and I will know that you can interpret it for me." The astrologers answered the king, "There is no one on earth who can do what the king asks! No king, however great and mighty, has ever asked such a thing of any magician or enchanter or astrologer. What the king asks is too difficult. No one can reveal it to the king except the gods, and they do not live among humans." This made the king so angry and furious that he ordered the execution of all the wise men of Babylon. So, the decree was issued to put the wise men to death, and men were sent to look for Daniel and his friends to put them to death. When Arioch, the commander of the king's guard, had gone out to put to death the wise men of Babylon, Daniel spoke to him with wisdom and tact. He asked the king's officer, "Why did the king issue such a harsh decree?" Arioch then explained the matter to Daniel. At this, Daniel went in to the king and asked for time, so that he might interpret the dream for him. Then Daniel returned to his house and explained the matter to his friends Hananiah, Mishael and Azariah. He urged them to plead for mercy from the God of heaven concerning this mystery, so that he and his friends might not be executed with the rest of the wise men of Babylon. During the night the mystery was revealed to Daniel in a vision. Then Daniel praised the God of heaven and said: "Praise be to the name of God for ever and ever; wisdom and power are his.

He changes times and seasons; he deposes kings and raises up others. He gives wisdom to the wise and knowledge to the discerning. He reveals deep and hidden things; he knows what lies in darkness, and light dwells with him. I thank and praise you, God of my ancestors:

You have given me wisdom and power, you have made known to me what we asked of you, you have made known to us the dream of the king." Then Daniel went to Arioch, whom the king had appointed to execute the wise men of Babylon, and said to him, "Do not execute the wise men of Babylon. Take me to the king, and I will interpret his dream for him." Arioch took Daniel to the king at once and said, "I have found a man among the exiles from Judah who can tell the king what his dream means." The king asked Daniel (also called Belteshazzar), "Are you able to tell me what I saw in my dream and interpret it?" Daniel replied, "No wise man, enchanter, magician or diviner can explain to the king the mystery he has asked about, but there is a God in heaven who reveals mysteries. He has shown King Nebuchadnezzar what will happen in days to come. Your dream and the visions that passed through your mind as you were lying in bed are these: "As Your Majesty was lying there, your mind turned to things to come, and the revealer of mysteries showed you what is going to happen. As for me, this mystery has been revealed to me, not because I have greater wisdom than anyone else alive, but so that Your Majesty may know the interpretation and that you may understand what went through your mind. "Your Majesty looked, and there before you stood a large statue—an enormous, dazzling statue, awesome in appearance. The head of the statue was made of pure gold, its chest and arms of silver, its belly and thighs of bronze, its legs of iron, its feet partly of iron and partly of baked clay. While you were watching, a rock was cut out, but not by human hands. It struck the statue on its feet of iron and clay and smashed them. Then the iron, the clay, the bronze, the silver and the gold were all broken to pieces and became like chaff on a threshing floor in the summer. The wind swept them away without leaving a trace. But the rock that struck the statue became a huge mountain and filled the whole earth. "This was the dream, and now we will interpret it to the king. Your Majesty, you are the king of kings. The God of heaven has given you dominion and power and might and glory; in your hands he has placed all mankind and the beasts of the field and the birds in the sky. Wherever they live, he has made you ruler over them all. You are that head of gold. "After you, another kingdom will arise, inferior to yours. Next, a third kingdom, one of bronze, will rule over the whole earth. Finally, there will be a fourth kingdom, strong as iron—for iron breaks and smashes everything—and as iron breaks things to pieces, so it will crush and break all the others. Just as you saw that the feet and toes were partly of baked clay and partly of iron, so this will be a divided kingdom; yet it will have some of the strength of iron in it, even as you saw iron mixed with clay. As the toes were partly iron and partly clay, so this kingdom will be partly strong and partly brittle. And just as you saw the iron mixed with baked clay, so the people will be a mixture and will not remain united, any more than iron mixes with clay. "In the time of those kings, the God of heaven will set up a kingdom that will never be destroyed, nor will it be left to another people. It will crush all those kingdoms and bring them to an end, but it will itself endure forever. This is the meaning of the vision of the rock cut out of a mountain, but not by human hands —a rock that broke the iron, the bronze, the clay, the silver and the gold to pieces. "*The great God has shown the king what will take place in the future. The dream is true and its interpretation is trustworthy.*" *Then King Nebuchadnezzar fell prostrate before Daniel and paid him honor and ordered that an offering and incense be presented to him. The king said to Daniel, "Surely your God is the God of gods and the Lord of kings and a revealer of mysteries, for you were able to reveal this mystery." [Daniel 2:1-47 NIV]*

"*In the first year of Belshazzar king of Babylon, Daniel had a dream, and visions passed through his mind as he was lying in bed. He wrote down the substance of his dream. Daniel said: "In my vision at night I looked, and there before me were the four winds of heaven churning up the great sea. Four great beasts, each different from the others, came up out of the sea. "The first was like a lion, and it had the wings of an eagle. I watched until its wings were torn off and it was lifted from the ground so that it stood on two feet like a human being, and the mind of a human was given to it. "And there before me was a second beast, which looked like a bear. It was raised up on one of its sides, and it had three ribs in its mouth between its teeth. It was told, 'Get up and eat your fill of flesh!' "After that, I looked, and there before me was another beast, one that looked like a leopard. And on its back, it had four wings like those of a bird. This beast had four heads, and it was given authority to rule. "After that, in my vision at night I looked, and there before me was a fourth beast—terrifying and frightening and very powerful. It had large iron teeth; it crushed and devoured its victims and trampled underfoot whatever was left. It was different from all the former beasts, and it had ten horns. "While I was thinking about the horns, there before me was another horn, a little one, which came up among them; and three of the first horns were uprooted before it. This horn had eyes like the eyes of a human being and a mouth that spoke boastfully. "As I looked, "thrones were set in place, and the Ancient of Days took his seat. His clothing was as white as snow; the hair of his head was white like wool. His throne was flaming with fire, and its wheels were all ablaze. A river of fire was flowing, coming out from before him. Thousands upon thousands attended him; ten thousand times ten thousand stood before him. The court was seated, and the books were opened. "Then I continued to watch because of the boastful words the horn was speaking. I kept looking until the beast was slain and its body destroyed and thrown into the blazing fire. (The other beasts had been stripped of their authority, but were allowed to live for a period of time.) "In my vision at night I looked, and there before me was one like a son of man, coming with the clouds of heaven. He approached the Ancient of Days and was led into his presence. He was given authority, glory and sovereign power; all nations and peoples of every language worshiped him. His dominion is an everlasting dominion that will not pass away, and his kingdom is one that will never be destroyed.*

"*I, Daniel, was troubled in spirit, and the visions that passed through my mind disturbed me. I approached one of those standing there and asked him the meaning of all this. "So, he told me and gave me the interpretation of these things: 'The four great beasts are four kings that will rise from the earth. But the holy people of the Most High will receive the kingdom and will possess it forever—yes, for ever and ever.'*

"*Then I wanted to know the meaning of the fourth beast, which was different from all the others and most terrifying, with its iron teeth and bronze claws—the beast that crushed and devoured its victims and trampled underfoot whatever was left. I also wanted to know about the ten horns on its head and about the other horn that came up, before which three of them fell—the horn that looked more imposing than the others and that had eyes and a mouth that spoke boastfully. As I watched, this horn was waging war against the holy people and defeating them, until the Ancient of Days came and pronounced judgment in favor of the holy people of the Most High, and the time came when they possessed the kingdom. "He gave me this explanation: 'The fourth beast is a fourth kingdom that will appear on earth. It will be different from all the other kingdoms and will devour the whole earth, trampling it down and crushing it. The ten horns are ten kings who will come from this kingdom. After them another king will arise, different from the earlier ones; he will subdue three kings. He will speak against the Most High and oppress his holy people and try to change the set times and the laws. The holy people will be delivered into his hands for a time, times and half a time. "'But the court will sit, and his power will be taken away and completely destroyed forever. Then the sovereignty, power and greatness of all the kingdoms under heaven will be handed over to the holy people of the Most High. His kingdom will be an everlasting kingdom, and all rulers will worship and obey him.' "This is the end of the matter. I, Daniel, was deeply troubled by my thoughts, and my face turned pale, but I kept the matter to myself." [Daniel 7:1-28 NIV]*

"In the third year of King Belshazzar's reign, I, Daniel, had a vision, after the one that had already appeared to me. In my vision I saw myself in the citadel of Susa in the province of Elam; in the vision I was beside the Ulai Canal. I looked up, and there before me was a ram with two horns, standing beside the canal, and the horns were long. One of the horns was longer than the other but grew up later. I watched the ram as it charged toward the west and the north and the south. No animal could stand against it, and none could rescue from its power. It did as it pleased and became great. As I was thinking about this, suddenly a goat with a prominent horn between its eyes came from the west, crossing the whole earth without touching the ground. It came toward the two-horned ram I had seen standing beside the canal and charged at it in great rage. I saw it attack the ram furiously, striking the ram and shattering its two horns. The ram was powerless to stand against it; the goat knocked it to the ground and trampled on it, and none could rescue the ram from its power. The goat became very great, but at the height of its power the large horn was broken off, and in its place four prominent horns grew up toward the four winds of heaven. Out of one of them came another horn, which started small but grew in power to the south and to the east and toward the Beautiful Land. It grew until it reached the host of the heavens, and it threw some of the starry host down to the earth and trampled on them. It set itself up to be as great as the commander of the army of the Lord; it took away the daily sacrifice from the Lord, and his sanctuary was thrown down. Because of rebellion, the Lord's people and the daily sacrifice were given over to it. It prospered in everything it did, and truth was thrown to the ground. Then I heard a holy one speaking, and another holy one said to him, "How long will it take for the vision to be fulfilled—the vision concerning the daily sacrifice, the rebellion that causes desolation, the surrender of the sanctuary and the trampling underfoot of the Lord's people?" He said to me, "It will take 2,300 evenings and mornings; then the

sanctuary will be reconsecrated." While I, Daniel, was watching the vision and trying to understand it, there before me stood one who looked like a man. And I heard a man's voice from the Ulai calling, "Gabriel, tell this man the meaning of the vision." As he came near the place where I was standing, I was terrified and fell prostrate. "Son of man," he said to me, "understand that the vision concerns the time of the end." While he was speaking to me, I was in a deep sleep, with my face to the ground. Then he touched me and raised me to my feet. He said: "I am going to tell you what will happen later in the time of wrath, because the vision concerns the appointed time of the end. The two-horned ram that you saw represents the kings of Media and Persia. The shaggy goat is the king of Greece, and the large horn between its eyes is the first king. The four horns that replaced the one that was broken off represent four kingdoms that will emerge from his nation but will not have the same power. "In the latter part of their reign, when rebels have become completely wicked, a fierce-looking king, a master of intrigue, will arise. He will become very strong, but not by his own power. He will cause astounding devastation and will succeed in whatever he does. He will destroy those who are mighty, the holy people. He will cause deceit to prosper, and he will consider himself superior. When they feel secure, he will destroy many and take his stand against the Prince of princes. Yet he will be destroyed, but not by human power. "The vision of the evenings and mornings that has been given you is true, but seal up the vision, for it concerns the distant future." I, Daniel, was worn out. I lay exhausted for several days. Then I got up and went about the king's business. I was appalled by the vision; it was beyond understanding." [Daniel 8:1-27 NIV]

From the inspired words of counsel revealed to Daniel, God shows;

- *The human kings and their kingdoms that would rule the world until the time of God's own king and His kingdom. The rise and fall of human kingdoms until divine kingdom is established. [Daniel 2:36-43 NIV]*
- *In the time of those kings, the God of heaven will set up a kingdom that will never be destroyed, nor will it be left to another people. It will crush all those kingdoms and bring them to an end, but it will itself endure forever. [Daniel 2:44 NIV]*
- *The son of man is the ultimate King of kings, coming with the clouds of heaven. He approached the Ancient of Days and was led into his presence. He was given authority, glory and sovereign power; all nations and peoples of every language worshiped him. His dominion is an everlasting dominion that will not pass away, and his kingdom is one that will never be destroyed. He is the rock cut out of a mountain, but not by human hands — a rock that broke the iron, the bronze, the clay, the silver and the gold to pieces. [Daniel 7:13-14 NIV]*
- *The holy people of the Most High will receive the kingdom and will possess it forever — yes, forever and ever. [Daniel 7:18 NIV]*

- ***Micah:***

"You, Bethlehem Ephrathah, though you are small among the clans of Judah, out of you will come for me one who will be ruler over Israel, whose origins are from of old, from ancient times." Therefore, Israel will be abandoned until the time when she who is in labor bears a son, and the rest of his brothers return to join the Israelites. He will stand and shepherd his flock in the strength of the Lord, in the majesty of the name of the Lord his God. And they will live securely, for then his greatness will reach to the ends of the earth. And he will be our peace." [Micah 5:2-5 NIV]

- ***Stephen,*** the 1st century martyr gave the summary of Israel's history and the plan of God for the people of the world as his defense when he was about to be stoned to death.

"The God of glory appeared to our father Abraham while he was still in Mesopotamia, before he lived in Harran. 'Leave your country and your people,' God said, 'and go to the land I will show you.' "So, he left the land of the Chaldeans and settled in Harran. After the death of his father, God sent him to this land where you are now living. He gave him no inheritance here, not even enough ground to set his foot on. But God promised him that he and his descendants after him would possess the land, even though at that time Abraham had no child. God spoke to him in this way: 'For four hundred years your descendants will be strangers in a country not their own, and they will be enslaved and mistreated. But I will punish the nation they serve as slaves,' God said, 'and afterward they will come out of that country and worship me in this place.' Then he gave Abraham the covenant of circumcision. And Abraham became the father of Isaac and circumcised him eight days after his birth. Later Isaac became the father of Jacob, and Jacob became the father of the twelve patriarchs. "Because the patriarchs were jealous of Joseph, they sold him as a slave into Egypt. But God was with him and rescued him from all his troubles. He gave Joseph wisdom and enabled him to gain the goodwill of Pharaoh king of Egypt. So Pharaoh made him ruler over Egypt and all his palace. "Then a famine struck all Egypt and Canaan, bringing great suffering, and our ancestors could not find food. When Jacob heard that there was grain in Egypt, he sent our forefathers on their first visit. On their second visit, Joseph told his brothers who he was, and Pharaoh learned about Joseph's family. After this, Joseph sent for his father Jacob and his whole family, seventy-five in all. Then Jacob went down to Egypt, where he and our ancestors died. Their bodies were brought back to Shechem and placed in the tomb that Abraham had bought from the sons of Hamor at Shechem for a certain sum of money.

"As the time drew near for God to fulfill his promise to Abraham, the number of our people in Egypt had greatly increased. Then 'a new king, to whom Joseph meant nothing, came to power in Egypt.' He dealt treacherously with our people and oppressed our ancestors by forcing them to throw out their newborn babies so that they would die.

"At that time Moses was born, and he was no ordinary child. For three months he was cared for by his family. When he was placed outside, Pharaoh's daughter took him and brought him up as her own

son. *Moses was educated in all the wisdom of the Egyptians and was powerful in speech and action.*
"When Moses was forty years old, he decided to visit his own people, the Israelites. He saw one of them
being mistreated by an Egyptian, so he went to his defense and avenged him by killing the Egyptian.
Moses thought that his own people would realize that God was using him to rescue them, but they did
not. The next day Moses came upon two Israelites who were fighting. He tried to reconcile them by saying,
'Men, you are brothers; why do you want to hurt each other?' "But the man who was mistreating the
other pushed Moses aside and said, 'Who made you ruler and judge over us? Are you thinking of killing
me as you killed the Egyptian yesterday?' When Moses heard this, he fled to Midian, where he settled as
a foreigner and had two sons. "After forty years had passed, an angel appeared to Moses in the flames of
a burning bush in the desert near Mount Sinai. When he saw this, he was amazed at the sight. As he
went over to get a closer look, he heard the Lord say: 'I am the God of your fathers, the God of Abraham,
Isaac and Jacob.' Moses trembled with fear and did not dare to look. "Then the Lord said to him, 'Take
off your sandals, for the place where you are standing is holy ground. I have indeed seen the oppression
of my people in Egypt. I have heard their groaning and have come down to set them free. Now come, I
will send you back to Egypt.' "This is the same Moses they had rejected with the words, 'Who made you
ruler and judge?' He was sent to be their ruler and deliverer by God himself, through the angel who
appeared to him in the bush. He led them out of Egypt and performed wonders and signs in Egypt, at
the Red Sea and for forty years in the wilderness. "This is the Moses who told the Israelites, 'God will
raise up for you a prophet like me from your own people.' He was in the assembly in the wilderness, with
the angel who spoke to him on Mount Sinai, and with our ancestors; and he received living words to
pass on to us. "But our ancestors refused to obey him. Instead, they rejected him and, in their hearts,
turned back to Egypt. They told Aaron, 'Make us gods who will go before us. As for this fellow Moses
who led us out of Egypt—we don't know what has happened to him!' That was the time they made an
idol in the form of a calf. They brought sacrifices to it and reveled in what their own hands had made.
But God turned away from them and gave them over to the worship of the sun, moon and stars. This
agrees with what is written in the book of the prophets: "'Did you bring me sacrifices and offerings forty
years in the wilderness, people of Israel? You have taken up the tabernacle of Molek and the star of your
god Rephan, the idols you made to worship. Therefore, I will send you into exile' beyond Babylon. "Our
ancestors had the tabernacle of the covenant law with them in the wilderness. It had been made as God
directed Moses, according to the pattern he had seen. After receiving the tabernacle, our ancestors under
Joshua brought it with them when they took the land from the nations God drove out before them. It
remained in the land until the time of David, who enjoyed God's favor and asked that he might provide
a dwelling place for the God of Jacob. But it was Solomon who built a house for him.

"However, the Most High does not live in houses made by human hands. As the prophet says:
"'Heaven is my throne, and the earth is my footstool. What kind of house will you build for me? says
the Lord.

Or where will my resting place be? Has not my hand made all these things?' "You stiff-necked people!

Your hearts and ears are still uncircumcised. You are just like your ancestors: You always resist the Holy Spirit! Was there ever a prophet your ancestors did not persecute? They even killed those who predicted the coming of the Righteous One. And now you have betrayed and murdered him — you who have received the law that was given through angels but have not obeyed it."" [Acts 7:2-53 NIV]

- *   **Paul** who was a 1st century writer, herald and minister, from Tarsus and had studied with Gamaliel, grew up in the Pharisaical order and from the tribe of Benjamin, he persecuted the people of the Way until he was chosen and appointed as a servant of the Lord to the Gentiles. He wrote, argued and defended certain important truths about the Lord Jesus Christ and His kingdom.

"Paul was waiting for them in Athens, his spirit was deeply disturbed to see the city full of idols. So, he began holding discussions in the synagogue with the Jews and other worshipers, as well as every day in the public square with anyone who happened to be there. Some Epicurean and Stoic philosophers also debated with him. Some asked, 'What is this blabbermouth trying to say?' while others said, 'He seems to be preaching about foreign gods.' This was because Paul was telling the good news about Jesus and the resurrection. Then they took him, brought him before the Areopagus, and asked, 'May we know what this new teaching of yours is? It sounds rather strange to our ears, and we would like to know what it means.' Now all the Athenians and the foreigners living there used to spend their time do nothing else other than listening to the latest ideas or repeating them.

So, Paul stood up in front of the Areopagus and said, 'Men of Athens, I see that you are very religious in every way. For as I was walking around and looking closely at the objects you worship, I even found an altar with this written on it: 'To an unknown god.' So, I am telling you about the unknown object you worship. The God who made the world and everything in it is the Lord of heaven and earth. He doesn't live in shrines made by human hands, and he isn't served by people as if he needed anything. He himself gives everyone life, breath, and everything else. From one man he made every nation of humanity to live all over the earth, fixing the seasons of the year and the national boundaries within which they live, so that they might look for God, somehow reach for him, and find him. Of course, he is never far from any one of us. For we live, move, and exist because of him, as some of your own poets have said: 'For we are his children, too.'

So, if we are God's children, we shouldn't think that the divine being is like gold, silver, or stone, or is an image carved by humans using their own imagination and skill. Though God has overlooked those times of ignorance, he now commands everyone everywhere to repent, because he has set a day when he is going to judge the world with justice through a man whom he has appointed. He has given proof of this to everyone by raising him from the dead.'

When they heard about a resurrection of the dead, some began joking about it, while others said, 'We will hear you again about this.' And so, Paul left the meeting. Some men joined him and became believers. With them were Dionysius, who was a member of the Areopagus, a woman named Damaris, and some others along with them." [Acts 17:16-34 NIV]

"I do not want you to be ignorant of the fact, brothers and sisters, that our ancestors were all under the cloud and that they all passed through the sea. They were all baptized into Moses in the cloud and in the sea. They all ate the same spiritual food and drank the same spiritual drink; for they drank from the spiritual rock that accompanied them, and that rock was Christ. Nevertheless, God was not pleased with most of them; their bodies were scattered in the wilderness.

Now these things occurred as examples to keep us from setting our hearts on evil things as they did. Do not be idolaters, as some of them were; as it is written: "The people sat down to eat and drink and got up to indulge in revelry." We should not commit sexual immorality, as some of them did—and in one day twenty-three thousand of them died. We should not test Christ, as some of them did—and were killed by snakes. And do not grumble, as some of them did —and were killed by the destroying angel.

These things happened to them as examples and were written down as warnings for us, on whom the culmination of the ages has come. So, if you think you are standing firm, be careful that you don't fall! No temptation has overtaken you except what is common to mankind. And God is faithful; he will not let you be tempted beyond what you can bear. But when you are tempted, he will also provide a way out so that you can endure it." [1 Corinthians 10:1-13 NIV]

"From: Paul, a servant of Jesus the Messiah, called to be an apostle and set apart for God's gospel, which he promised beforehand through his prophets in the Holy Scriptures regarding his Son. He was a descendant of David with respect to his humanity and was declared by the resurrection from the dead to be the powerful Son of God according to the Spirit of holiness -Jesus the Messiah, our Lord." [Romans 1:1-6 ISV]

Every detail of the person of Jesus Christ was prepared and written by the Law and the Prophets before their reality was seen in His life, He came precisely to fulfill every word spoken and written.

CHAPTER FIVE

The Fullness of Time:

The time of Reformation and the New Order, The Reality over The Shadow, The Last Man.

All that were happening, all the series of events were all to culminate into the *fullness of time*. It was placing things in the exact manner for the Ancient of Days to reveal His ultimate and only plan for all of humanity. He was now ready to set in the *new order*, the *time of reformation* and to reveal the *real substance* of all things. For the time of formation had come and passed, the age of deformation was happening, and the age of reformation needed to be fulfilled, the time to re-work all that was destroyed and initiate the age of conformation. It was the set time for the world and all creation to witness the grand agenda of God.

"Concerning this salvation, the prophets, who spoke of the grace that was to come to you, searched intently and with the greatest care, trying to find out the time and circumstances to which the Spirit of Christ in them was pointing when he predicted the sufferings of the Messiah and the glories that would follow. It was revealed to them that they were not serving themselves but you, when they spoke of the things that have now been told you by those who have preached the gospel to you by the Holy Spirit sent from heaven. Even angels long to look into these things." [1 Peter 1:10-12 NIV]

"When the set time had fully come, God sent his Son, born of a woman, born under the law, to redeem those under the law." [Galatians 4:4 NIV]

When the apostle Paul wrote to the Galatian churches to correct the errors of falling from grace, and when he also wrote to the Romans and other churches about being under the law and under grace, the usual meaning of the word *the law* that he used referred to; *the laws of Mount Sinai with its variables on mount Moab and mount Horeb; its curses, blessings, prescribed works, commandment, requirements and ordinances,* he often termed it as *the old covenant*. This is different from when he used terms like; the *law of sin and death*, the *law of Spirit of life*, the *law of the mind* and so on.

The redemption of man was the most impossible mission made possible, it is the greatest manifestation of God's purposes, plans, principles, process, personality, power and pleasure. It is the mission about how, God;

- *Came to earth from heaven.*
- *Became a man and lived as a man.*
- *The creator came to the creation.*
- *The creator became the created.*
- *Died, physically and spiritually.*
- *Forsook Himself.*
- *Rose from the dead.*
- *Exchanged life for death and righteousness for sin for man.*
- *Negotiated for the release of mankind from hostage of sin and death.*

By the redemption, God was placing His last card, His only option available. There was and could be no other way or means apart from it.

God's redemption of man was, He redeeming man from:

- *The hand and power of the enemy.*
- *The wilderness and the wander lands, the power of destitution and distress.*
- *The darkness, shadow of death and gates of hades.*
- *The hard-bitter labor of living.*
- *The rebellion of man.*

God's redemption of man was He restoring man to:

- *The image and likeness of Him.*
- *The rulership over all creation.*
- *The original place and position of glory and honor.*
- *The blessing of His promise and covenant to Abraham.*
- *The fulfillment of the sworn oath of eternal reign of the seed of David.*

The Law and Prophets Fulfilled:
A peculiar phrase that Jesus Christ used was that;
"Do not think that I have come to ABOLISH the Law or the Prophets; I have not come to abolish them but to FULFILL them." ~ Jesus of Nazareth [Matthew 5:17 NIV]
What did He mean by such statement? What was the Law and the Prophets, why had He not come to abolish them but to fulfill them? The Law is a term used to represent the record of writings

by Moses and the Prophets refers to the records of the prophets of ancient Israel. In these records were prophecies about the coming Messiah who would be the ultimate man to fulfill the counsel of the God of Israel. To *ABOLISH* means to *annul, abrogate, end the effect* of something, to *FULFILL* means to *satisfy, complete, execute, comply with, and make do on* a cause, an assignment or a work. Jesus Christ came to satisfy, complete, and execute everything that was written about Him by the Law and the Prophets.

"Now the birth of Jesus the Messiah happened in this way. When his mother Mary was engaged to Joseph, before they lived together, she was discovered to be pregnant by the Holy Spirit. Her husband Joseph, being a righteous man and unwilling to disgrace her, decided to divorce her secretly. After he had thought about it, an angel of the Lord appeared to him in a dream and said," Joseph, son of David, don't be afraid to take Mary as your wife, because what has been conceived in her is from the Holy Spirit. She will give birth to a son, and you are to name him Jesus, because he is the one who will save his people from their sins." Now all this happened to FULFILL what was declared by the Lord through THE PROPHET when he said, "See, a virgin will become pregnant and give birth to a son, and they will name him Immanuel," which means, "God with us."

When Joseph got up from his sleep, he did as the angel of the Lord had commanded him and took Mary as his wife. He did not have marital relations with her until she had given birth to a son; and he named him Jesus." [Matthew 1:18-25 NIV]

"After Jesus had been born in Bethlehem of Judea in the days of King Herod, wise men from the east arrived in Jerusalem and asked," Where is the one who was born king of the Jews? We saw his star in the east and have come to worship him." When King Herod heard this, he was disturbed, as was all of Jerusalem. He called together all the high priests and scribes of the people and asked them where the Messiah was to be born. They told him, "In Bethlehem of Judea, because that is what was written by THE PROPHET: 'O Bethlehem in the land of Judah, you are by no means least among the rulers of Judah, because from you will come a ruler who will shepherd my people Israel.'"

Then Herod secretly called together the wise men, found out from them the time the star had appeared, and sent them to Bethlehem. He told them," As you go, search carefully for the child. When you find him, tell me so that I, too, may go and worship him." After listening to the king, they set out, and the star they had seen in the east went ahead of them until it came and stopped over the place where the child was. When they saw the star, they were ecstatic with joy. After they went into the house and saw the child with his mother Mary, they fell down and worshiped him. Then they opened their treasure sacks and offered him gifts of gold, frankincense, and myrrh. Having been warned in a dream not to go back to Herod, they left for their own country by a different road. After they [the wise men who visited the born king] had gone, an angel of the Lord appeared to Joseph in a dream and said, "Get up, take the child and his mother, and flee to Egypt. Stay there until I tell you, because Herod intends to search for the child and kill him."

So, Joseph got up, took the child and his mother, and left at night for Egypt. He stayed there until

Herod's death in order to FULFILL what was declared by the Lord through THE PROPHET when he said," Out of Egypt I called my Son." When Herod saw that he had been tricked by the wise men, he flew into a rage and ordered the execution of all the male children in Bethlehem and all its neighboring regions who were two years old and younger, according to the time that he had determined from the wise men. Then what was declared by THE PROPHET Jeremiah was FULFILLED when he said, "A voice was heard in Ramah: wailing and great mourning. Rachel was crying for her children. She refused to be comforted, because they no longer existed."

But after Herod died, an angel of the Lord appeared in a dream to Joseph in Egypt and said, "Get up, take the child and his mother, and go to the land of Israel, because those who were trying to kill the child are dead." So, Joseph got up, took the child and his mother, and went into the land of Israel. But when he heard that Archelaus was ruling over Judea in place of his father Herod, he was afraid to go there. After having been warned in a dream, he left for the region of Galilee and came and settled in a town called Nazareth in order to FULFILL what was said by THE PROPHETS:" He will be called a Nazarene." [Matthew 2:1-23 NIV]

"Now when Jesus heard that John had been arrested, he went back to Galilee. He left Nazareth and went and settled in Capernaum by the sea, in the regions of Zebulun and Naphtali, in order to FULFILL what was declared by THE PROPHET Isaiah when he said,

"O Land of Zebulun and Land of Naphtali, on the road to the sea, across the Jordan, Galilee of the Gentiles! The people living in darkness have seen a great light, and for those living in the land and shadow of death, a light has risen."

From then on, Jesus began to preach and to say, "Repent, because the kingdom of heaven is near!" [Matthew 4:12-17 NIV]

"Then I said, 'Here I am — it is written about me in the scroll — I have come to do your will, my God.'" [Hebrews 10:7 NIV]

"When Jesus went into Peter's house, he saw Peter's mother-in-law lying in bed, sick with a fever. He touched her hand, and the fever left her. Then she got up and began serving him. When evening came, people brought to him many who were possessed by demons. He drove out the spirits by speaking a command and healed everyone who was sick. This was to FULFILL what was declared by THE PROPHET Isaiah when he said, "It was he who took our illnesses away and removed our diseases." [Matthew 8:14-17 NIV]

"When Jesus became aware of this, he left that place. Many crowds followed him, and he healed all of them, ordering them not to make him known. This was to FULFILL what was declared by THE PROPHET Isaiah when he said, "Here is my Servant whom I have chosen, whom I love, and with whom I am pleased! I will put my Spirit on him, and he will proclaim justice to the gentiles. He will not quarrel or shout, and no one will hear him shouting in the streets. He will not snap off a broken reed or snuff out a smoldering wick until he has brought justice through to victory. And in his name the gentiles will hope." [Matthew 12:15-21 NIV]

"Jesus told the crowds all these things in parables. He did not tell them anything without using a parable. This was to FULFILL what was declared by THE PROPHET when he said, "I will open my mouth to speak in parables. I will declare what has been hidden since the creation of the world." [Matthew 13:34-35 NIV]

A very vital event happened in the life of Peter, James and John when the master led them to the high mountain one day, on the mountain, the master's appearance transfigured, His clothes dazzling white, whiter than anyone in the world could bleach. In such an atmosphere, there appeared before them Elijah and Moses who were talking with the master. Amazed and frightened at what he was seeing, Peter said to the master; *"Rabbi, it is good for us to be here. Let us put up three shelters—one for you, one for Moses and one for Elijah." [He did not know what to say, they were so frightened.] [Matthew 17:4 NIV]*

For the purposes of this meeting not to be missed a cloud appeared, covering them and a voice came from the cloud saying; *"This is my Son, whom I love. Listen to him!" [Matthew 17:5 NIV]*

After Peter, James and John has heard the voice from the cloud they could see no one else except Jesus, upon their return from the mountain, Jesus ordered them not to tell anyone of what they saw until the Son of Man had risen from the dead, so they kept the matter to themselves whiles they kept on discussing what *"rising from the dead"* meant. So they asked Jesus; *"Why do the teachers of the law say that Elijah must come first?" [Matthew 17:10 NIV]* Jesus answered their question but also asked them a question of His own, He said; *"To be sure, Elijah does come first, and restores all things. [Matthew 17:11 NIV] Why then is it WRITTEN that the Son of Man must suffer much and be rejected? [Mark 8:31 NIV] But I tell you, Elijah has come, and they have done to him everything they wished, just as it is WRITTEN about him [the Elijah who had come]." [Matthew 17:12 NIV]* By His reply, the disciples understood that He was talking about John the Baptist. *[Matthew 17:13 NIV]* This event was important and significant because it was setting the case to validate and confirm the resurrection and the return of the Lord as written by the Law and the Prophets. In this meeting, two dead men came physically alive and talked with one physically living man whiles three physically living men observed, this established that in the mouth of two or more witness the testimony about the resurrection and the return would be sure. That is why the three witnesses were discussing what rising from the dead meant. This is the prophecy about the coming first of Elijah and the Messiah; *"Surely the day is coming; it will burn like a furnace. All the arrogant and every evildoer will be stubble, and the day that is coming will set them on fire," says the Lord Almighty. "Not a root or a branch will be left to them. But for you who revere my name, the sun of righteousness will rise with healing in its rays. And you will go out and frolic like well-fed calves. Then you will trample on the wicked; they will be ashes under the soles of your feet on the day when I act," says the Lord Almighty. "Remember the law of my servant Moses, the decrees and laws I gave him at Horeb for all Israel. "See, I will send the prophet Elijah to you before that great and dreadful day of the Lord comes. He will turn the hearts of the parents to their children, and the hearts of the children to their parents; or else I will come and strike the land with total destruction." [Malachi 4:1-6 NIV]*

Let us continue to look at other scriptures that talks of Jesus coming and being the fulfillment of the Law and the Prophets.

"As they approached Jerusalem and came to Bethphage on the Mount of Olives, Jesus sent two disciples, saying to them, "Go to the village ahead of you, and at once you will find a donkey tied there, with her colt by her. Untie them and bring them to me. If anyone says anything to you, say that the Lord needs them, and he will send them right away." This took place to FULFILL what was spoken through THE PROPHET "Say to Daughter Zion, 'See, your king comes to you, gentle and riding on a donkey, and on a colt, the foal of a donkey.'" [Zechariah 9:9] The disciples went and did as Jesus had instructed them. They brought the donkey and the colt and placed their cloaks on them for Jesus to sit on. A very large crowd spread their cloaks on the road, while others cut branches from the trees and spread them on the road. The crowds that went ahead of him and those that followed shouted, "Hosanna to the Son of David!" "Blessed is he who comes in the name of the Lord!" "Hosanna in the highest heaven!" [Psalm 118:25, 26] When Jesus entered Jerusalem, the whole city was stirred and asked, "Who is this?" The crowds answered, "This is Jesus, the prophet from Nazareth in Galilee." [Matthew 21:1-11 NIV]

"They took palm branches and went out to meet him, shouting,

"Hosanna!" "Blessed is he who comes in the name of the Lord!"

"Blessed is the king of Israel!" Jesus found a young donkey and sat on it, as it is written: "Do not be afraid, Daughter Zion; see, your king is coming, seated on a donkey's colt." ("Rejoice greatly, Daughter Zion!

Shout, Daughter Jerusalem! See, your king comes to you, righteous and victorious, lowly and riding on a donkey, on a colt, the foal of a donkey. I will take away the chariots from Ephraim and the warhorses from Jerusalem, and the battle bow will be broken. He will proclaim peace to the nations. His rule will extend from sea to sea and from the River to the ends of the earth.") At first his disciples did not understand all this. Only after Jesus was glorified did they realize that these things had been WRITTEN about him and that these things had been done to him." [John 12:12-16 NIV]

The Principle:

- *The Law and the Prophets were the "containers" with the "content" that was to be revealed. Jesus is that "content".*
- *Whiles Jesus Christ Himself was alive, He told His disciples and the people of His generation that everything must be fulfilled that was written about Him in the Law of Moses, the Prophets and the Psalms. [Luke 24:44 NIV]*
- *Jesus is the arrival of the servant chosen king, the son of man, seed of David. Jesus is the king that brought back from heaven the kingdom of God, He brought back to the earth the influence,*

nature, government, dominion, order and manifestation of God. The name of Jesus is the hope of the gentiles, all of the human race must place our hope in Christ Jesus.

- *Jesus Christ fulfilled and would fulfill every one of the Law and the Prophet word written about Him. "Truly I tell you, until heaven and earth disappear, not the smallest letter, not the least stroke of a pen, will by any means disappear from the Law until everything is accomplished." [Matthew 5:18 NIV] Jesus will achieve completely and successfully the Law and Prophets.*

The Stone the Builders Rejected: A Word to the Unborn Ones, the Future Generation.

When you enter into this world, where ever your location by family, community, society or nation, and whenever your time, there would be the *builders of the age,* by their social wisdom and traditional knowledge they would reject you, by their understanding of building, you would not fit their structure and form, so you would become rejected by them but there is hope for you. In the ancient quarries of the Hebrew people, highly-trained stonemasons were carefully choosing the stones to construct the temple of the living God. These master builders inspected the many stones available to them, and selected the ones they wanted according to their expertise, yet they rejected one particular stone that did not suit their purpose and this very rejected stone became the cornerstone, the most important of all the stone, when after putting up their structure they finally realized that the position of the cornerstone was missing and the only stone that fitted that position was the first stone that they had rejected they had to go for this stone. Without the cornerstone the integrity of the whole structure was compromised and the structure could not stand line by line, everything else became depended on that rejected but now cornerstone, capstone; *the last to the first stone.* This happened because the hand of the Lord was involved and acted on behalf of the stone that was rejected, this stone was and is Christ Jesus, He Himself said to the chief priests and the Pharisees of His generation who rejected Him, *"Have you never read in the Scriptures: "'The stone the builders rejected has become the cornerstone; the Lord has done this, and it is marvelous in our eyes'"" [Matthew 21:42, Psalm 118:22-23 NIV]* Just as Jesus Christ was rejected by the builders but became the cornerstone by the doing of the Lord and He became marvelous in the eyes of all in heaven and on earth so also when they reject you, you would become the cornerstone by the doing of the Lord and be marvelous in the eyes of your generation. Just as Jesus Christ became the stone that was laid in Zion as the scriptures said; *"Look! I am laying a chosen, precious cornerstone in Zion. The one who believes in him will never be ashamed." [Isaiah 28:16 NIV]* Believe in Him as the chosen precious capstone and you will never be ashamed, for He would make you also a chosen precious capstone. The right hand of the Lord would do mighty things! In you, the right hand of the Lord would lift you high; the right hand of the Lord would do mighty things! And you would live in your generation to proclaim what the Lord has done.

The CROSS.

The cross was not an option for Jesus, it was the necessity, the cup He must drink to purchase the freedom and salvation of humanity. There was no way round this cup, the cup that He needed to drink to release man from the wrath of God. It was not an accident for Jesus but a divine incident to fulfill divine purposes.

"Just as Moses lifted up the snake in the wilderness, so the Son of Man must be lifted up, that everyone who believes may have eternal life in him." [John 3:14-15 NIV]

"Jesus said, "When you have lifted up the Son of Man, then you will know that I am he and that I do nothing on my own but speak just what the Father has taught me. The one who sent me is with me; he has not left me alone, for I always do what pleases him." [John 8:28-29 NIV]

Jesus replied, "The hour has come for the Son of Man to be glorified. Very truly I tell you, unless a kernel of wheat falls to the ground and dies, it remains only a single seed. But if it dies, it produces many seeds. Anyone who loves their life will lose it, while anyone who hates their life in this world will keep it for eternal life. Whoever serves me must follow me; and where I am, my servant also will be. My Father will honor the one who serves me.

"Now my soul is troubled, and what shall I say? 'Father, save me from this hour'? No, it was for this very reason I came to this hour. 28 Father, glorify your name!" Then a voice came from heaven, "I have glorified it, and will glorify it again." The crowd that was there and heard it said it had thundered; others said an angel had spoken to him. [John 12:23-29 NIV]

"Jesus said, "This voice was for your benefit, not mine. Now is the time for judgment on this world; now the prince of this world will be driven out. And I, when I am lifted up from the earth, will draw all people to myself." He said this to show the kind of death he was going to die. The crowd spoke up, "We have heard from the Law that the Messiah will remain forever, so how can you say, 'The Son of Man must be lifted up'? Who is this 'Son of Man'?" Then Jesus told them, "You are going to have the light just a little while longer. Walk while you have the light, before darkness overtakes you. Whoever walks in the dark does not know where they are going. Believe in the light while you have the light, so that you may become children of light." When he had finished speaking, Jesus left and hid himself from them." [John 12:30-36 NIV]

The people of Israel sinned against God in the desert and were infested with incurable venomous snake bites. They cried to God and He responded to heal them by mounting a bronze serpent on a pool, and everyone who looked up to the bronze serpent on the pool was restored completely.

"They traveled from Mount Hor along the route to the Red Sea, to go around Edom. But the people grew impatient on the way; they spoke against God and against Moses, and said, "Why have you brought us up out of Egypt to die in the wilderness? There is no bread! There is no water! And we detest this miserable food!"

Then the Lord sent venomous snakes among them; they bit the people and many Israelites died. The people came to Moses and said, "We sinned when we spoke against the Lord and against you. Pray that the Lord will take the snakes away from us." So, Moses prayed for the people. The Lord said to Moses, "Make a snake and put it up on a pole; anyone who is bitten can look at it and live." So, Moses made a bronze snake and put it up on a pole. Then when anyone was bitten by a snake and looked at the bronze snake, they lived."[Numbers 21:4-9 NIV]

We see from these that while the people were suffering from the penalty of their sins, their salvation for their suffering came from looking at the bronze serpent on the pool.

All of humanity has been bitten by the deception of the snake that resulted in one man's sin and therefore all man sinned. We all are under the venomous bite of sin. And it is only by looking at the lifted Son of Man on the cross are we cured of sin and live; *look and live,* look to Christ on the cross and live.

Again, it was only by the means of the cross could the Son of Man be crucified to fulfill all the requirements of death and pay fully the penalty of sin. And it was only during the times of the Roman Empire that the act of killing by crucifixion was perfected to meet the standard of God as stated by the Spirit of God through David in order to fulfill His eternal ultimate redemption plan;

"I waited patiently for the Lord; he turned to me and heard my cry. He lifted me out of the slimy pit, out of the mud and mire; he set my feet on a rock and gave me a firm place to stand. He put a new song in my mouth, a hymn of praise to our God. Many will see and fear the Lord and put their trust in him. Blessed is the one who trusts in the Lord, who does not look to the proud, to those who turn aside to false gods? Many, Lord my God, are the wonders you have done, the things you planned for us. None can compare with you; was I to speak and tell of your deeds, they would be too many to declare? Sacrifice and offering you did not desire — but my ears you have opened — burnt offerings and sin offerings you did not require. Then I said, "Here I am, I have come — it is written about me in the scroll. I desire to do your will, my God; your law is within my heart." I proclaim your saving acts in the great assembly; I do not seal my lips, Lord, as you know. I do not hide your righteousness in my heart; I speak of your faithfulness and your saving help. I do not conceal your love and your faithfulness from the great assembly. Do not withhold your mercy from me, Lord; may your love and faithfulness always protect me. For troubles without number surround me; my sins have overtaken me, and I cannot see. They are more than the hairs of my head, and my heart fails within me. Be pleased to save me, Lord; come quickly, Lord, to help me. May all who want to take my life be put to shame and confusion; may all who desire my ruin be turned back in disgrace. May those who say to me, "Aha! Aha!" be appalled at their own shame. But may all who seek you rejoice and be glad in you; may those who long for your saving help always say, "The Lord is great!" But as for me, I am poor and needy; may the Lord think of me. You are my help and my deliverer; you are my God, do not delay." [Psalm 40:1-17 NIV]

In this psalter, the psalmist presented various aspects of the workings of the cross of Christ, let us look at the imagery that he used to depict the picture of Christ's cross for humanity.

Cry: *The cry of the psalmist was also the cry of the human race, which also became the cry of Christ* *on the cross. As a result of sin, mankind was in a pit of confusion, a slimy pit in which we were sinking for it is muddy and miry. Our cry was and is a cry for a savior, when the Lord lifted man out of this pit, he set the feet of man on a rock, the firm place to stand, who or what is this rock? That the one who trusts in Him as the Lord, and does not look to the proud, to those who turn aside to false gods can have assurance in? [Psalm 40:1-2 and 40:4 NIV]*

Compare: *The rock is this man in whom the Lord had planned to demonstrate His wonders through, of which He has done, such that the things planned for the human race through this rock none can compare with, it is of these wonderful things we are exploring and speaking, to tell of His deeds, even though they are too many to declare. [Psalm 40:5 NIV]*

Cross: *The requirements of the Lord is righteousness, faithfulness, mercy, and love in the deep places of the heart, but due to sin, innumerable evils, troubles without number surround the human race; sins overtakes our life such that we cannot see even what evil is. The ills of our world are more than the hairs on our head, and our heart fails within us. That which is required to satisfy this desire of the Lord truthfully and graciously is a true sacrifice and offering not animal sacrifice and offering neither is it burnt offerings and sin offerings, so in order for His requirement to be meet and His desire fulfilled, the Lord Himself prepared a body to sacrifice and offer for the sin of man. The ears of this body was opened to hear the voice of the Lord, to be obedient to it and the heart of this body was ready, desiring to do the will of God, so God installed His law in that heart, this body came to do everything that was written about Him in the scroll of the Lord. On the cross the body was fulfilling the desires and requirements of God, far beyond any imagination of the human heart or the understating of the human minds. [Psalm 40:12 NIV]*

Come: *The time had come for the saving act of God to be shown, so He came by the power of the cross. The Lord who is great! had come to man who was poor and needy; the awesome Lord had now brought His thoughts of thinking about man to man, the helper and deliverer; God, had not delayed nor abandoned man but had come to help and deliver. [Psalm 40:17 NIV]*

Conceal: *The pleasure of God was now on display on the cross, He was pleased to save man on the cross by the crucifixion of His Son, by His revealed love and faithfulness, He was now protecting man, and throwing all who sort for the life of man into confusion and shame, the destroyer who demanded for the ruin of man was turned back in disgrace. On the cross, God demonstrated His love and faithfulness, He revealed what pleases Him and there is nothing else that can be done about it or to it by anyone or anything. [Psalm 40:13-14 NIV]*

"My God, my God, why have you forsaken me? Why are you so far from saving me, so far from my cries of anguish? My God, I cry out by day, but you do not answer, by night, but I find no rest. Yet you are enthroned as the Holy One; you are the one Israel praises. In you our ancestors put their trust; they trusted and you delivered them. To you they cried out and were saved; in you they trusted and were not put to shame. But I am a worm and not a man, scorned by everyone, despised by the people. All who see me mock me; they hurl insults, shaking their heads. "He trusts in the Lord," they say, "let the Lord rescue

him. Let him deliver him, since he delights in him." Yet you brought me out of the womb; you made me trust in you, even at my mother's breast. From birth I was cast on you; from my mother's womb you have been my God. Do not be far from me, for trouble is near and there is no one to help. Many bulls surround me; strong bulls of Bashan encircle me. Roaring lions that tear their prey open their mouths wide against me. I am poured out like water, and all my bones are out of joint. My heart has turned to wax; it has melted within me. My mouth is dried up like a potsherd, and my tongue sticks to the roof of my mouth; you lay me in the dust of death. Dogs surround me, a pack of villains encircles me; they pierce my hands and my feet. All my bones are on display; people stare and gloat over me. They divide my clothes among them and cast lots for my garment. But you, Lord, do not be far from me. You are my strength; come quickly to help me. Deliver me from the sword, my precious life from the power of the dogs. Rescue me from the mouth of the lions; save me from the horns of the wild oxen. I will declare your name to my people; in the assembly I will praise you. You who fear the Lord, praise him! All you descendants of Jacob, honor him! Revere him, all you descendants of Israel! For he has not despised or scorned the suffering of the afflicted one; he has not hidden his face from him but has listened to his cry for help. From you comes the theme of my praise in the great assembly; before those who fear you, I will fulfill my vows. The poor will eat and be satisfied; those who seek the Lord will praise him—may your hearts live forever! All the ends of the earth will remember and turn to the Lord, and all the families of the nations will bow down before him, for dominion belongs to the Lord and he rules over the nations. All the rich of the earth will feast and worship; all who go down to the dust will kneel before him—those who cannot keep themselves alive. Posterity will serve him; future generations will be told about the Lord. They will proclaim his righteousness, declaring to a people yet unborn: He has done it!" [Psalm 22:1-30 NIV]

My God, My God: *The greatest question of the human heart in our world is the question of abandonment, the question of if there is God, then why has He abandoned us, why does this happen or that happen which in our eyes is evil and wicked. It is as if we as a people are forsaken in our cries of anguish, in groaning words throughout our days and nights without any answer. Such was the anguish that was inflicted on the Son by the Father on the cross. The Son was in anguish for all of mankind, He was experiencing the Fathers rejection for the sake of humanity, He was forsaken for my sake, for your sake, in His forsaken state, we are made: free from every evil, reconciled, restored, revived, to the Father, one with the Father, sons of the Father, accepted by the Father, access to the Father and exalted by the Father. [Psalm 22:1-2 NIV]*

My heart, My mouth -- Man: *The man on the cross was turned into a "worm" by the disfigurement infliction on Him on the cross in extreme pain, He no longer resembled a man but like a worm. He was reduced to the form of a worm by the evil treatment meted out to Him on the cross. Sin had made man to be like a worm and in order to deliver man from the worm state, He had to be reduced to same, as water is poured from a jar of clay so was he poured out, all His bones are out of joint, dismembered on display by piercing His hands and His feet with blood overflowing. His heart melted within Him like the wax does in the presence of heat such that His strength was dried up like a potsherd, and His* tongue stacked to the roof of His mouth so He cannot speak; He was brought down and laid in the dust of death – the grave in the earth. [Psalm 22:6, 14-15 NIV]

Many: *The myriad of forces of wickedness and darkness both physical and spiritual were all active around the cross, even casting lots among themselves for His garment and clothes, like bulls they surrounded Christ; they encircled His soul like strong bulls. They opened their mouth wide, roaring like lions to tear Him up as their prey, as a pack of dogs they surrounded Him, but all to no avail for they were only but a pack of villains. The sword could not kill him, nor take His precious life, the power of the dogs, the mouth of the lions and the horns of the wild oxen could not devour nor destroy Him and by the cross He has released mankind from their grip and control. [Psalm 22:12-13, 16, 18, 20-21 NIV]*

Power from the Christ's Cross:

"Save me, O God, for the waters have come up to my neck. I sink in the miry depths, where there is no foothold. I have come into the deep waters; the floods engulf me. I am worn out calling for help; my throat is parched. My eyes fail, looking for my God. Those who hate me without reason outnumber the hairs of my head; many are my enemies without cause, those who seek to destroy me. I am forced to restore what I did not steal. You, God, know my folly; my guilt is not hidden from you. Lord, the Lord Almighty, may those who hope in you not be disgraced because of me; God of Israel, may those who seek you not be put to shame because of me. For I endure scorn for your sake, and shame covers my face. I am a foreigner to my own family, a stranger to my own mother's children; for zeal for your house consumes me, and the insults of those who insult you fall on me. When I weep and fast, I must endure scorn; when I put on sackcloth, people make sport of me. Those who sit at the gate mock me, and I am the song of the drunkards. But I pray to you, Lord, in the time of your favor; in your great love, O God, answer me with your sure salvation. Rescue me from the mire, do not let me sink; deliver me from those who hate me, from the deep waters. Do not let the floodwaters engulf me or the depths swallow me up or the pit close its mouth over me. Answer me, Lord, out of the goodness of your love; in your great mercy turn to me. Do not hide your face from your servant; answer me quickly, for I am in trouble. Come near and rescue me; deliver me because of my foes. You know how I am scorned, disgraced and shamed; all my enemies are before you. Scorn has broken my heart and has left me helpless; I looked for sympathy, but there was none, for comforters, but I found none. They put gall in my food and gave me vinegar for my thirst. May the table set before them become a snare; may it become retribution and a trap. May their eyes be darkened so they cannot see, and their backs be bent forever. Pour out your wrath on them; let your fierce anger overtake them. May their place be deserted; let there be no one to dwell in their tents. For they persecute those you wound and talk about the pain of those you hurt. Charge them with crime upon crime; do not let them share in your salvation. May they be blotted out of the book of life and not be listed with the righteous. But as for me, afflicted and in pain—may your salvation, God, protect me. I will praise God's name in song and glorify him with thanksgiving. This will please the Lord more than *an ox, more than a bull with its horns and hooves. The poor will see and be glad —you who seek God, may your hearts live! The Lord hears the needy and does not despise his captive people. Let heaven and earth praise him, the seas and all that move in them, for God will save Zion and rebuild the cities of Judah. Then people will settle there and possess it; the children of his servants will inherit it, and those who love his name will dwell there." [Psalm 69:1-36 NIV]*

Sufferings, Sin--king and Stranger: *The power of the cross of Christ is that, Christ suffered for all the sufferings of humanity, He went through suffering for mankind, telling us that even in and through suffering there is success in the end. It was through the cross that Jesus suffered the ultimate of all His sufferings, as the waters of suffering engulfs the neck of the world so also Jesus Christ was engulfed with the human suffering to His neck, as man sinks in the miry depths of sin and death, where there is no foothold so Christ on the cross sunk into sin and death for man in order to gain a foothold for man. He came into the deep waters, the floods that swells up man and He brought man out of them, He heard the worn-out call for help of the ranks of man such that our throat are parched and on the cross, He called out for help from the Father for man. With our failing eyes looking for God, He came to give us light to see God truly. Those who hated Him without reason outnumbered the hairs of His head; many were His enemies without cause, those who sort to destroy Him, He became a stranger to His own mother's children. [Psalm 69:1-4, 8 NIV]*

Scoffers, Scorn and Sackcloth: *Man is faced with scoffs and scorns in this lifetime, Jesus Christ was scoffed by the scoffers for the scoffed in life, and with ridicule and insult they disdained the Son of God on the cross. He endured scorn for our sake, and disgrace covered His face on behalf of the face of man, the insults of those who insult God fell on Him on the cross. The drunkards who sat at the gate mocked Him, and He became their song. Scorn broke His heart and left Him helpless as all the enemies were before Him; He looked for sympathy, but there was none, for comforters, but He found none. They placed gall in His food and gave Him vinegar for His thirst. [Psalm 69:7, 9, 11-12 NIV]*

Shame and Sacrifice: *If you wanted to shame a person in the culture of the Romans, crucify him. If you wanted to curse someone according to the law of the ancient Jewish, hang him on a pole. Whiles human culture and laws were shaming and cursing the Lord Jesus Christ by the cross, the Almighty was presenting His sacrifice that takes away the sin of the world, the disobedience of all of humanity. He sacrificed Himself to save man from Himself and save man unto Himself. Man was charged with crime upon crime; such that man was to be blotted out of the book of life and not to be listed with the righteous, we were not to share in salvation but by the afflicted man on the cross, Christ, the pains He suffered made it possible for us to share in such a great salvation, the table set before man became a snare for us; it became our retribution and trap, our eyes even darkened so that we could not see, and our backs were bent forever. The wrath of God was poured on us; His fierce anger overtook us, our place was deserted; no one dwelled in our tents but by the persecution of the one that God wounded and the pain of the one that He hurt, we now have no charge of crime, our life is listed with the righteous, snare is released, our* *eyes are enlightened, our backs straightened, and we have peace with God and a place of dwelling in Him. [Psalm 69:22-26 NIV]*

Sure Salvation, Save: *By the cross of Christ, there is a sure salvation for all of mankind, if any man calls on the power of the cross, He will save, if any man cries out for the power of the cross, He will deliver, if any one commits to the power of the cross, He will not put the one to shame or disgrace. All who seek God will not be put to shame because of the power of the cross, for by the cross, Christ endured scorn for your sake, and shame covered His face so that shine could and would cover yours. By the cross, the rescue mission of the Lord Jesus Christ, He has rescued all of humanity from the miry mud and the flood waters. He has rescued all of mankind from the pit of confusion, the pit of death, the pit of debt, the pit of destruction and the pit of despair and dejection, He has rescued mankind from the forces of evil, because even the mouth of the well could not be shut at Him. He came out of the depths of the heart of the earth as the mighty one. [Psalm 69:1-3 NIV]*

Forced of Folly, Foreigner to Family, Favor of Face: *On the cross, Christ was treated as a thief, He was accused of "stealing kingship" as the king of the Jews, and He was forced to restore the kingship of humanity that He did not steal. He had no folly but was made to pay for the folly of mankind, He was guiltless yet was exposed on the cross to pay for the guilt of the human race that was not hidden from the judge of the universe. Lord, the Lord Almighty, became a foreigner to His own family – the Israelites; the zeal for the house – family, creation, mankind – of the Lord Almighty consumed Him to accomplish the work for which He was sent, so that out of the goodness of the Lord's love; in His great mercy, in the time of His favor; in His great love, He would turn to man on behalf of Christ. [Psalm 69:8-9 NIV]*

Poor to Prosper, Posterity to Proclaim Praise: *By the cross of Christ, God did not hide His face from His servant; but He answered Him quickly, from the trouble He was in for man. His Spirit came near and rescued Him; delivered Him because of the foes. By His, God's face is not hidden from man, and He is ever ready to answer and quickly deliver man from the foes, such that all those who hope in Him will not be disgraced because of Christ; those who seek the God of Israel, will not be put to shame because of Christ. The poor will see the power of the cross of Christ and be glad — those who seek God, their hearts live! The Lord hears the needy and does not despise His captive people in Christ. For they praise God's name in song and glorify Him with thanksgiving. This pleases the Lord more than an ox, more than a bull with its horns and hooves. Let heaven and earth praise Him, the seas and all that move in them, for God saved Zion and rebuild the cities of Judah by Christ through the cross. Then people will settle there and possess it; the children of His servants will inherit it, and those who love His name will dwell there. [Psalm 69:17-18, 32-36 NIV]*

The Message of the Cross.

The message from the cross is that it is finished, mercy has completed what it started before the foundations of the world. On the cross, the Most High God showed mercy on mankind.

Jesus Christ is the help that He sent from heaven to vindicate humanity. On the cross, God was demonstrating His love and faithfulness of truthfulness, He showed His great love that reaches to the heavens, His faithfulness that extends to the skies. He was exalting His glory above all of the earth by the broad casting message of the cross. He was being faithful and true to His word to redeem mankind. His love for righteousness and justice has brought Him to the point of being a sacrifice of atonement for all who dwell under the shadow of His wings and take refuge in Him. His righteousness which is like the highest mountains and His justice which is also like the great deep were being demonstrated to the universe. His priceless precious unfailing love was being served to man, so that man can feast on the abundance of His house, by the cross, He was and is inviting man back to the great banquet, calling man to come and drink from His river of delights – the Spirit – which is the fountain of life so that in His light man will see light. The message of the cross is that God is showing favor and restoring fortunes, He is forgiving sin because He has covered it all! He was setting aside all of His wrath and turning from all of His fierce anger on all who take refuge in the atoning sacrifice. He was restoring life because His anger is not forever and He was not going to prolong it through all generations, He was reviving man again so that man can rejoice in Him. The message the radio of the cross is broadcasting to world is that, God's wrath has been paid for in full and He is showing us His gracious love, He is granting salvation to and for all. His promises of peace is now available to His people and the sure salvation is near for all so that His glory will dwell in them all because love and faithfulness met together on the cross whiles righteousness and peace kissed each other, with faithfulness springing forth from the earth and righteousness looking down from heaven on humanity. Therefore, now righteousness goes before the Lord to prepare the ways for His steps to give us what is good and make our land fruitful, yield its harvest.

"He forgave us all our sins, having canceled the charge of our legal indebtedness, which stood against us and condemned us; he has taken it away, nailing it to the cross. And having disarmed the powers and authorities, he made a public spectacle of them, triumphing over them by the cross." [Colossians 2:13-15 NIV]

"The word of the Lord is right and true; he is faithful in all he does. The Lord loves righteousness and justice; the earth is full of his unfailing love." [Psalm 33:4-5 NIV]

"Your love, Lord, reaches to the heavens, your faithfulness to the skies. Your righteousness is like the highest mountains, your justice like the great deep. You, Lord, preserve both people and animals. How priceless is your unfailing love, O God! People take refuge in the shadow of your wings. They feast on the abundance of your house; you give them drink from your river of delights. For with you is the fountain of life; in your light we see light. Continue your love to those who know you, your righteousness to the upright in heart." [Psalm 36:5-10 NIV]

"Have mercy on me, my God, have mercy on me, for in you I take refuge. I will take refuge in the shadow of your wings until the disaster has passed. I cry out to God Most High, to God, who vindicates me. He sends from heaven and saves me, rebuking those who hotly pursue me— God sends forth his love

and his faithfulness. I am in the midst of lions; I am forced to dwell among ravenous beasts— men whose teeth are spears and arrows, whose tongues are sharp swords. Be exalted, O God, above the heavens; let your glory be over all the earth. They spread a net for my feet — I was bowed down in distress. They dug a pit in my path— but they have fallen into it themselves. My heart, O God, is steadfast, my heart is steadfast; I will sing and make music. Awake, my soul! Awake, harp and lyre! I will awaken the dawn. I will praise you, Lord, among the nations; I will sing of you among the peoples. For great is your love, reaching to the heavens; your faithfulness reaches to the skies. Be exalted, O God, above the heavens; let your glory be over all the earth." [Psalm 57:1-11 NIV]

"You, Lord, showed favor to your land; you restored the fortunes of Jacob. You forgave the iniquity of your people and covered all their sins. You set aside all your wrath and turned from your fierce anger.

Restore us again, God our Savior, and put away your displeasure toward us. Will you be angry with us forever? Will you prolong your anger through all generations? Will you not revive us again, that your people may rejoice in you? Show us your unfailing love, Lord, and grant us your salvation. I will listen to what God the Lord says; he promises peace to his people, his faithful servants— but let them not turn to folly. Surely his salvation is near those who fear him, that his glory may dwell in our land. Love and faithfulness meet together; righteousness and peace kiss each other. Faithfulness springs forth from the earth, and righteousness looks down from heaven. The Lord will indeed give what is good, and our land will yield its harvest. Righteousness goes before him and prepares the way for his steps." [Psalm 85:1-13 NIV]

The principles:

- *Jesus did it all on the cross, it is finished.*
- *Duty done, debt discharged, damage darned and deed deemed!*
- *Jesus came that He will break every curse hanging over humanity. He purchased freedom from the curse of the Law through the crucifixion on the Cross.*

C: — Christ, covenant, creation, church, counsel.
R: — redemption, restoration, reconciliation, revival, resurrection
O: — offering, offenses, obligation, obsolete.
S: — sacrifice, submission, shame, shed, sin.
S: — scourge, scorn, suffering, satisfy, success.

The Tomb.

The tomb was also not bypassed, He had to enter the grave and the mouth of Sheol and Hades. The place of death is a realm that does not give up the souls that it holds, its power to hold souls there is sin, the realm of death and destruction keeps captives of its captors. And its "ruler, god or king" is the devil. After death on the cross, the next place for Jesus Christ was the realm of death and destruction.

"Do not say in your heart, 'Who will ascend into heaven?' [that is, to bring Christ down] or Who will descend into the deep?' [that is, to bring Christ up from the dead]." [Romans 10:6-7 NIV]

"Who will ascend into heaven to get it and proclaim it to us so we may obey it?" Nor is it beyond the sea, so that you have to ask, "Who will cross the sea to get it and proclaim it to us so we may obey it?" [Deuteronomy 30:12-13 NIV]

Scripture says: "When he ascended on high, he took many captives and gave gifts to his people." What does "he ascended" mean except that he also descended to the lower, earthly regions? He who descended is the very one who ascended higher than all the heavens, in order to fill the whole universe. [Ephesians 4:8-10 NIV]

Descend or Ascend: *To descend, Jesus descended into the deep regions of the universe, the lower parts of the earth. He crossed beyond the sea, to the dead, the place of death and the realm of destruction. To declare, He went with the message He held and proclaimed to them, He declared the message of eternal redemption by Him, He preached the good message of deliverance to all righteous souls held and kept bound. His message on the cross was "it is finished", [John 19:30 NIV] every debt of sin is paid, every duty of justice is done and every desire of the Almighty is fulfilled, now sin has no control over your spirit, soul and body. To defend, He went before the ruler of the realm of death and darkness and made His case of victory, the enemy's charge of condemnation against man for disobedience was annulled. Because He Himself had paid for it fully and fulfilled the justice and righteousness of God Most High. To defeat, He defeated the powers that be, took hold of their authority, and disarmed them of their strength. All authority and power became subject to Him. He triumphed over them all. To deliver, now the time of deliverance has come for any righteous soul kept bound by the power of death and its ruler. The righteous souls that sin, death and the devil had kept captive were now delivered, freed and so is everyone who believes in Christ.*

To ascend, He rose from the dead by the power of the Spirit of God. The place of the death could not keep Him down, bind Him by its chains, He overcame its force and power by the divine mighty working of the Spirit of God to resurrect and He entered into heaven. Upon His ascension, He took captivities captive, He led captors in His triumphal procession, receiving gifts from people and giving gifts to people. "When you ascended on high, you took many captives; you received gifts from people, even from the rebellious — that you, Lord God, might dwell there. Praise be to the Lord, to God our Savior, who daily bears our burdens. Our God is a God who saves; from the Sovereign Lord comes escape from death. Surely God will crush the heads of his enemies, the hairy crowns of those who go on in their sins. The Lord says, "I will bring them from Bashan; I will bring them from the depths of the sea, that your feet may wade in the blood of your foes, while the tongues of your dogs have their share. Your procession, God, has come into view, the procession of my God and King into the sanctuary. In front are the singers, after them the musicians; with them are the young women playing the timbrels."" [Psalm 68:18-25 NIV]

The Triumphs of the Tomb:

"Keep me safe, my God, for in you I take refuge. I say to the Lord, "You are my Lord; apart from you I have no good thing." I say of the holy people who are in the land, "They are the noble ones in whom is all my delight." Those who run after other gods will suffer more and more.

I will not pour out libations of blood to such gods or take up their names on my lips. Lord, you alone are my portion and my cup; you make my lot secure. The boundary lines have fallen for me in pleasant places; surely I have a delightful inheritance. I will praise the Lord, who counsels me; even at night my heart instructs me. I keep my eyes always on the Lord.

With him at my right hand, I will not be shaken. Therefore, my heart is glad and my tongue rejoices; my body also will rest secure, because you will not abandon me to the realm of the dead, nor will you let your faithful one sees decay. You make known to me the path of life; you will fill me with joy in your presence, with eternal pleasures at your right hand." [Psalm 16:1–11 NIV]

"In you, LORD, I have taken refuge; let me never be put to shame. In your righteousness, rescue me and deliver me; turn your ear to me and save me. Be my rock of refuge, to which I can always go; give the command to save me, for you are my rock and my fortress. Deliver me, my God, from the hand of the wicked, from the grasp of those who are evil and cruel. For you have been my hope, Sovereign LORD, my confidence since my youth. From birth I have relied on you; you brought me forth from my mother's womb. I will ever praise you. I have become a sign to many; for my enemies speak against me; those who wait to kill me conspire together. They say, "God has forsaken him; pursue him and seize him, for no one will rescue him." Do not be far from me, my God; come quickly, God, to help me. I will come and proclaim your mighty acts, Sovereign Lord; I will proclaim your righteous deeds, yours alone. Since my youth, God, you have taught me, and to this day I declare your marvelous deeds. Even when I am old and gray, do not forsake me, my God, till I declare your power to the next generation, your mighty acts to all who are to come. Your righteousness, God, reaches to the heavens, you who have done great things. Who is like you, God? Though you have made me see troubles, many and bitter, you will restore my life again; from the depths of the earth you will again bring me up. You will increase my honor and comfort me once more." [Psalm 71:1-23 NIV]

Refugee of Presence, Rejoice in Praise, Right of Path, Rest in Pleasure, Realm to Portion:
The issues of life is not limited to only this life time, it goes beyond, the human heart desires safety, significance and satisfaction both in this life and beyond. All areas of our life is expressed in these areas of safety, significance and satisfaction, we want to be secured; secured from loses, harm and others, we want to be significant; to matter in this matter of life, to be important and valuable, now and forever and finally we want to have satisfaction; we want to be satisfied in life and living with long and good life. Our greatest challenge to these is death and what happens next, some of us demise death and after life all together but the tomb of Christ gives a different picture and meaning to this question of life and

death. We are as a race, are all seeking for a place of refuge, a place of security, a place of strength and a place of success; testament to this is the many gods to whom we run after, yet we suffer more and more — the gods of religion, rites, rituals, culture, customs. We pour out "libations of blood" to such gods or take up their names on our lips to no effectual ends. The Psalmist realizing this need, identified the person in whom to go to for such a place; he recognized this person as "my God, my Lord", in whom he took refuge and apart from Whom he had no good thing, such that he told of it to the holy people who were in the land, the noble ones in whom were all his delight that they also must take refuge in the God, the Lord, for without Him they also had no good thing. [Psalm 16:1-4 NIV] Why was the psalmist full of assurance in this God and Lord? What was his reason for such total trust? he had come to understand that, the Lord would not abandon him in the realm of dead, nor would the Lord allow His faithful one see decay for the Lord would make known to him the path of life and fill him with joy in His presence, with eternal pleasures at His right hand, the psalmist became sure that the Lord would bring him back from the dead and place him in the Lord's presence forever with eternal pleasures to satisfy him, so with such confidence, he would in this life time keep his eyes always on the Lord, his heart would be glad in the Lord and his tongue would rejoice in Him because his body would rest secured in the hand of the God Lord. Again the Lord alone was his portion and his cup; the one who makes his lot secure such that the boundary lines fall for him in pleasant places; and he surely had a delightful inheritance. For with the Lord at his right hand, he would not be shaken. He has taken refuge in Him; so he would never be put to shame, In the Lord's righteousness, He would rescue him and deliver him; turning His ear to him to save him. The Lord had become His rock of refuge, to which he always go; the Lord's command He gives would save him, for the Lord is his rock and fortress. So He asked his God to deliver him from the hand of the wicked, from the grasp of those who are evil and cruel. And because the Sovereign LORD is his hope, confidence and reliance form his youth and from birth in his mother's womb. [Psalm 16:10-11 NIV]

The principles-

- *The dead could not hold Jesus Christ down. [Acts 2:24 NIV]*
- *Jesus Christ rose form the death! [Luke 24:6 NIV]*
- *Those in live in Jesus Christ will also rise again after death. [John 11:25 NIV]*

The Throne.

The tomb leads Christ and all in Christ to the throne, to the place of ruler and dominion in His kingdom. The throne marks the ultimate reality of the purpose and power of Christ. By the cross, He went into the tomb, by the tomb, He went to the throne.

"The Lord says to my lord: "Sit at my right hand until I make your enemies a footstool for your feet." The Lord will extend your mighty scepter from Zion, saying, "Rule in the midst of your enemies!" Your troops will be willing on your day of battle. Arrayed in holy splendor, your young men will come to you

like dew from the morning's womb. The Lord has sworn and will not change his mind: "You are a priest forever, in the order of Melchizedek." The Lord is at your right hand; he will crush kings on the day of his wrath. He will judge the nations, heaping up the dead and crushing the rulers of the whole earth. He will drink from a brook along the way, and so he will lift his head high." [Psalm 110:1-7 NIV]

My Right Hand: *Christ Jesus is honored with the right hand position on the throne, the seat of kingdom government, where He is the "right hand man" due to the work He finished on the cross, and in the tomb. He is honored above all else with glory beyond measure and with grandeur splendor. [Psalm 110:1 NIV]*

Mighty Scepter: *Jesus Christ's scepter of and for rulership is mighty, it is the scepter of might held in His right hand extended from the center of His kingdom, Zion, to rule in the midst of all His enemies until all of them become His footstool; they all are subject to His dominion authority. [Psalm 110:2 NIV]*

Morning's Womb: *like dew from the morning's womb, the dew that has the freshness of strength and the firmness of splendor at the beginning of beginnings of birth so are the young men who come to Christ on the holy mountain --Zion-- as willing troops on His day of battle, they would be arrayed in holy majesty. [Psalm 110:3 NIV]*

Mind Made Up: *The Lord's mind is made up, He has taken an oath and sworn that Christ is the priest forever in the order of Melchizedek. Christ is king of peace and king of righteousness eternally. He is the priest who sits and serves as the righteous king from everlasting to everlasting. [Psalm 110:4 NIV]*

Mighty Warrior: *Jesus Christ at the Lord's right hand is the king – priest who rules over all, the Lord is at Jesus Christ's right hand as the mighty warrior who conquers and executes judgment over all – nations; kings and rulers, peoples and the whole earth. He cannot be defeated in battle on the day of His wrath for His head would be lifted up high after the day of battle. [Psalm 110:5 NIV]*

"The king rejoices in your strength, Lord. How great is his joy in the victories you give! You have granted him his heart's desire and have not withheld the request of his lips. You came to greet him with rich blessings and placed a crown of pure gold on his head. He asked you for life, and you gave it to him— length of days, for ever and ever. Through the victories you gave, his glory is great; you have bestowed on him splendor and majesty. Surely you have granted him unending blessings and made him glad with the joy of your presence. For the king trusts in the Lord; through the unfailing love of the Most High he will not be shaken. Your hand will lay hold on all your enemies; your right hand will seize your foes. When you appear for battle, you will burn them up as in a blazing furnace. The Lord will swallow them up in his wrath, and his fire will consume them. You will destroy their descendants from the earth, their posterity from mankind. Though they plot evil against you and devise wicked schemes, they cannot succeed. You will make them turn their backs when you aim at them with drawn bow. Be exalted in your strength, Lord; we will sing and praise your might." [Psalm 21:1-13 NIV]

Request: *The king Jesus, made request of the Lord, His heart desires He expressed on His lips to the Lord, He asked for life, length of days forever and ever. [Psalm 21:2-4 NIV]*

Rise Up: *He received these requests, when He rose up, He received victories upon victories such that the plot of evil against Him and the devises of wicked schemes upon Him, could not succeed. [Psalm 21:11 NIV]*

Right Hand: *His right hand seized His foes, when He appeared for battle, He burned them up as in a blazing furnace and swallowed them up in His wrath, and His fire consumed them. [Psalm 21:8-9 NIV]*

Riches: *such that He gained greater glory; He was bestowed with splendor and majesty, a crown of pure gold was placed on His head. He was granted unending rich blessings due to the unfailing love of the Most High and made glad with the joy of the Lord's presence. [Psalm 21:5-6 NIV]*

Rejoice: *therefore, the king rejoices in the Lord's strength, His joy is great in the victories He was given! [Psalm 21:1 NIV]*

"The earth and everything in it exist for the LORD – the world and those who live in it. Indeed, he founded it upon the seas, he established it upon deep waters. Who may ascend the mountain of the LORD?

Who may stand in his holy place? The one who has innocent hands and a pure heart; the person who does not delight in what is false and does not swear an oath deceitfully. This person will receive blessing from the LORD and righteousness from the God of his salvation.

This is the generation that seeks him. Those who seek your face are the true seed of Jacob. Lift up your heads, gates! Be lifted up, ancient doors, so the King of Glory may come in. Who is the King of Glory? The LORD strong and mighty, the LORD, mighty in battle.

Lift up your heads, gates! Be lifted up, ancient doors, so the King of Glory may come in. Who is he, this King of Glory? The LORD of the heavenly armies – He is the King of Glory." [Psalm 24:1-10 NIV]

The Lord: *The LORD for whom the earth and everything in it exists for, because He founded it upon the seas and established it upon the deep water, and indeed, He created the world and those who live in it came to the world and those people who live in it, the question is why did He come to the world and to those who live in it?, the psalmist answered this question with his own questions and answer. [Psalm 24:1-2 NIV]*

The One: *the psalmist asked of who may ascend the mountain of the LORD and who may stand in His holy place? [Psalm 24:3 NIV] The mountain of the LORD is the place of habitation and the dwelling of the presence and power of the LORD, it is the HOLY PLAC E of the LORD. The psalmist asked the question because the demand for ascending and standing in the Holy place of the Lord is pure innocent hands – righteousness outside and pure clean heart – righteousness inside. Such a person does not delight in what is false and does not swear an oath deceitfully, he does not lift up his soul into vanity. But the problem is that since the fall of man due to disobedience, every human's heart is unclean and hands are dirty, hence no man could ascend and stand in the Holy place of the Lord. The Lord then came to the world and those in it to make their hearts pure and their hands clean by His blood and life, so that as He has ascended to the mountain of the LORD and is standing in the Holy place of the Lord all who* *are in Him can also ascend and stand in the holy place. For this to happen, this person must seek the Lord who came to the world and become a new generation by receiving blessing from the LORD and righteousness from the God of His salvation. [Psalm 24:3-4 NIV]*

The Gates – Ancient Doors: *when the LORD left the heaven and entered into the earth world, when from the bosom of eternity, He dawned into time and blossomed in the womb of time, all the gates bowed down their heads to look into time, the ancient doors were lowered to see what is happening in the earth world. So when He finished His work and needed to ascend back to the Holy place with the new generation of the ranks of mankind who were captives in His captivity, the gates had to lift up their heads! The ancient doors had to be also lifted up, so that the King of Glory could enter in. The King of Glory is the LORD strong and mighty, the LORD, mighty in battle, He, this King of Glory is the LORD of the heavenly armies – He is the King of Glory. [Psalm 24:7-10 NIV]*

The Tenants of the Throne Room.

"Christ also suffered once for sins, the righteous for the unrighteous, to bring you to God. He was put to death in the body but made alive in the Spirit. After being made alive, he went and made proclamation to the imprisoned spirits — to those who were disobedient long ago when God waited patiently in the days of Noah while the ark was being built. In it only a few people, eight in all, were saved through water, and this water symbolizes baptism that now saves you also—not the removal of dirt from the body but the pledge of a clear conscience toward God. It saves you by the resurrection of Jesus Christ, who has gone into heaven and is at God's right hand — with angels, authorities and powers in submission to him." [1 Peter 3:18-22 NIV]

"The heavens praise your wonders, Lord, your faithfulness too, in the assembly of the holy ones. For who in the skies above can compare with the Lord? Who is like the Lord among the heavenly beings? In the council of the holy ones God is greatly feared; he is more awesome than all who surround him. Who is like you, Lord God Almighty? You, Lord, are mighty, and your faithfulness surrounds you. You rule over the surging sea; when its waves mount up, you still them. You crushed Rahab like one of the slain; with your strong arm you scattered your enemies. The heavens are yours, and yours also the earth; you founded the world and all that is in it. You created the north and the south; Tabor and Hermon sing for joy at your name. Your arm is endowed with power; your hand is strong, your right hand exalted. Righteousness and justice are the foundation of your throne; love and faithfulness go before you. Blessed are those who have learned to acclaim you, who walk in the light of your presence, Lord. They rejoice in your name all day long; they celebrate your righteousness. For you are their glory and strength, and by your favor you exalt our horn. [Psalm 89:5-17 NIV].

"The Lord reigns, let the earth be glad, let the distant shores rejoice.

Clouds and thick darkness surround him; righteousness and justice are the foundation of his throne. Fire goes before him and consumes his foes on every side. His lightning lights up the world; the earth sees and trembles. The mountains melt like wax before the Lord, before the Lord of all the earth. The heavens proclaim his righteousness, and all peoples see his glory." [Psalm 97:1-6 NIV]

Assembly Awesome Almighty: *In the council of the holy ones of the heavenly beings, none comes close in comparison to and with the Almighty, first of all, all the powers of all the heavenly and the beings therefore and from Him, for Him and by Him. He is Almighty! Again He is awesome! Awesome without peer or company of comparison, none is like Him. [Psalm 89:6-7 NIV]*

Above, Among, Arm: *The Almighty is above and beyond all, He is faithful, righteous, just, loving in all His word, works and ways. Among all, He is above and His arm is mighty in strength and salvation. The people of the Lord must rejoice for He Christ is seated on high on their behalf. [Psalm 145:1-21 NIV]*

Reverence:

Due to what the Lord Jesus Christ has done, He is to be revered by all, served by all and acknowledged by all. His reverence is un-parallel and beyond measure. Service to Him must be unquestionable and acknowledging Him is not an option for any human being but a necessity. [Psalm 22:27-31ISV]

Remembrance:

A promise given to Him for the fulfillment of His divine assignment was that His name will be remembered by all nations, in all the nation. And sure, the promised is being fulfilled. He is remembered by all. His name is great in all the earth. [Psalm 45:17 ISV]

Ruler ship and Reign:

This kingdom stretches from shore to shore, till the sun rises and sets no more. He rules over all affairs in the heavens and the earth, all counsels are under the authority of His name. [Psalm 72:7-10 NIV]

The principles-

- *Jesus Christ is seated on high in majesty and He reigns by His righteous scepter. [Psalm 45:6, 110:1-2 ISV]*
- *Jesus Christ has power over the grave, over the realm of death and destruction. [Revelation 1:18 ISV]*
- *Jesus Christ holds all the keys of life and death. [Revelation 1:18 ISV]*

The Return.

Once again, the Spirit of the Lord inspired the psalmist David and Asaph to describe the return of the Lord of Lords for the final solution to all things in the last time. The final salvation and judgment of all things. That which occurred in the life of David with his foes, and also the events of time in the people of Israel as recorded by Asaph tell of the future picture of the King of Kings' victory over all His defeated foes and judgment over all nations; kings and rulers.

"I love you, Lord, my strength. The Lord is my rock, my fortress and my deliverer; my God is my rock, in whom I take refuge, my shield and the horn of my salvation, my stronghold. I called to the Lord, who is worthy of praise, and I have been saved from my enemies. The cords of death entangled me; the torrents of destruction overwhelmed me. The cords of the grave coiled around me; the snares of death confronted me. In my distress I called to the Lord; I cried to my God for help. From his temple he heard my voice; my cry came before him, into his ears. The earth trembled and quaked, and the foundations of the mountains shook; they trembled because he was angry. Smoke rose from his nostrils; consuming fire came from his mouth, burning coals blazed out of it. He parted the heavens and came down; dark clouds were under his feet. He mounted the cherubim and flew; he soared on the wings of the wind. He made darkness his covering, his canopy around him— the dark rain clouds of the sky. Out of the brightness of his presence clouds advanced, with hailstones and bolts of lightning. The Lord thundered from heaven; the voice of the Most High resounded. He shot his arrows and scattered the enemy, with great bolts of lightning he routed them. The valleys of the sea were exposed and the foundations of the earth laid bare at your rebuke, Lord, at the blast of breath from your nostrils. He reached down from on high and took hold of me; he drew me out of deep waters. He rescued me from my powerful enemy, from my foes, who were too strong for me. They confronted me in the day of my disaster, but the Lord was my support. He brought me out into a spacious place; he rescued me because he delighted in me. The Lord has dealt with me according to my righteousness; according to the cleanness of my hands he has rewarded me. For I have kept the ways of the Lord; I am not guilty of turning from my God. All his laws are before me; I have not turned away from his decrees. I have been blameless before him and have kept myself from sin. The Lord has rewarded me according to my righteousness, according to the cleanness of my hands in his sight. To the faithful you show yourself faithful, to the blameless you show yourself blameless, to the pure you show yourself pure, but to the devious you show yourself shrewd. You save the humble but bring low those whose eyes are haughty. You, Lord, keep my lamp burning; my God turns my darkness into light." [Psalm 18:1-28 NIV]

Love of the Lord: *In the initial coming of the Lord, He came to serve His love to the world, in the final coming of the Lord, He is coming to seek His love of and from the world. The Lord came to be the rock, the fortress, and the deliverer for His love; so that He would be the God, the rock, in whom* *those who love Him would take refuge, in order to be their shield, the horn of their salvation, and their stronghold from this time and forever. [Psalm 18:1-2 NIV]*

Call of the Lord: *Humanity's call on the Lord from generation to generation has had one message of conversation, the message to Him in the distress call is that, the cords of death entangles us, the torrents of destruction overwhelms us and the cords of the grave coils around us, as the snares of death confronts us daily, nothing the might and means of man had done has been able to defeat death neither would it be able to do so. So we called for help from above to above, now in the finial coming of the Lord, He would end the sting of death ones for all and that of the power of the law of death. [Psalm 18:4-5 NIV]*

Coming of the Lord: *The Lord hears the call and responds accordingly at just the right time, from His temple in heaven, He hears the voice of man, the cry of the race is before Him and enters into His ears, then, and He decides to show forth. In the anger of the Lord at the state of demise of the human race, He has created being subjected to the sting of death by the oppressor, His anger causes the earth to tremble and quake, the foundations of the mountains shakes and trembles, smoke rising from His nostrils, consuming fire coming from His mouth, burning coal blazing out of it to devour death and the one who holds its power. He parts the heavens and comes down with dark clouds under His feet, He mounts the cherubim and flies soaring on the wings of the wind, He comes with His heavenly host of armies, making darkness His covering and the canopy around Him being the dark rain clouds in the sky. Out of the brightness of his presence, clouds of heavenly hosts would advance, with hailstones and bolts of lightning. The Lord would thunder from heaven; the voice of the Most High would resound in all of the universe one more time since the beginning of creation. He would shoot His arrows and scatter the enemy, with great bolts of lightning He would route them, and exposing the valleys of the sea and laying bare the foundations of the earth at the blast of breath from His nostrils. [Psalm 18:16-15 NIV]*

Reaching of the Lord: *The Lord would reach down from on high and take hold of His beloved ones; He would draw them out of deep waters and rescue them from their powerful enemy, from the foes of the age, the violent one, who are too strong for them. The Lord delights in His people and would reach down to rescue them from the enemy that confronts them in the day of disaster, bringing them out into a spacious place because He is their support in life. The Lord who lives! The Rock! The Exalted God! The Savior! He is the God who avenges humanity. [Psalm 18:16-19 NIV]*

Righteousness of the Lord: *At the coming and return of the Lord, He would deal with man according to righteousness, His dealing of judgment with man would be based on righteousness; He is going to show Himself faithful to those who are faithful with Him, to show Himself blameless to those who are blameless before Him, to show Himself pure to those who are pure in His sight but to the devious He would show Himself shrewd. [Psalm 18:25-26 NIV]*

Reward of the Lord: *The way of God is perfect, the word of the Lord is flawless; no one is God besides the Lord and no one is Rock except God and He shields all who take refuge in Him. He rewards them according to "their righteousness", the cleanness of their hands. The reward is based on the righteousness that they gain as they turn to God in Christ such that they are not guilty of turning from*

God, turning from His laws and away from His decrees. The reward for blamelessness before Him and having been kept from sin. For He rewards the humble with His salvation and those haughty in their eyes He rewards with lowness. He rewards the righteous by keeping their lamps burning; and turning their darkness into light, arming them with strength and keeping their way secure. At the return of the Lord, He would reward His righteous ones and the wicked as well.

[Psalm 18:27-28 NIV]

"The Mighty One, God, the Lord, speaks and summons the earth from the rising of the sun to where it sets. From Zion, perfect in beauty, God shines forth. Our God comes and will not be silent; a fire devours before him, and around him a tempest rages. He summons the heavens above, and the earth, that he may judge his people: "Gather to me this consecrated people, who made a covenant with me by sacrifice." And the heavens proclaim his righteousness, for he is a God of justice, "Listen, my people, and I will speak; I will testify against you, Israel: I am God, your God. I bring no charges against you concerning your sacrifices or concerning your burnt offerings, which are ever before me. I have no need of a bull from your stall or of goats from your pens, for every animal of the forest is mine, and the cattle on a thousand hills. I know every bird in the mountains, and the insects in the fields are mine. If I were hungry, I would not tell you, for the world is mine, and all that is in it. Do I eat the flesh of bulls or drink the blood of goats? "Sacrifice thank offerings to God, fulfill your vows to the Most High, and call on me in the day of trouble; I will deliver you, and you will honor me." But to the wicked person, God says: "What right have you to recite my laws or take my covenant on your lips? You hate my instruction and cast my words behind you. When you see a thief, you join with him; you throw in your lot with adulterers. You use your mouth for evil and harness your tongue to deceit. You sit and testify against your brother and slander your own mother's son. When you did these things and I kept silent, you thought I was exactly like you. But I now arraign you and set my accusations before you. "Consider this, you who forget God, or I will tear you to pieces, with no one to rescue you: Those who sacrifice thank offerings honor me, and to the blameless I will show my salvation." [Psalm 50:1-23 NIV]

The Mighty One: *The Lord would shine forth from Zion, the perfection of beauty upon His return, the Mighty One, God, the Lord, would speak and summon the earth from the rising of the sun to where it sets, He would come and would not be silent; a fire would devour before Him, and around Him a tempest would rage. He would summon the heavens above, and the earth, that He may judge His people. [Psalm 50:1-4 NIV]*

The Consecrated Ones: *He would gather "this" [Psalm 50:5 NIV] consecrated people, who have made a covenant with me by sacrifice, the covenant by the sacrifice of Himself on the cross – the new covenant. As the God of justice, the heavens proclaim His righteousness, so He would summon the heavens as witness of His judgment, Himself would speak and testify against His people, His testimony of accusation is not about matters of sacrifices, concerning burnt offerings, the sacrifice of material things* *to God. These sacrifices are not His concern because He created them all and have no need or desire of them to be satisfied with and by them being offered. [Psalm 50:6-8 NIV]*

The Wicked Ones: *Rather His charge of crime is about the injustice and wickedness of the wicked. He questions the right of the wicked to recite His laws or take up His covenant on their lips whiles they hate His instructions and cast His words behind Him, they join in the theft of the thief and throw lots with adulterers, they use their mouth for evil and harness their tongue for deceit, sitting and testifying against a fellow brother whiles slandering. The wicked think that God is exactly like them since in their acts He kept silent. But He would now arraign them and set His accusations before them, He tells them who forget God to consider or He would tear them to pieces, with no one to rescue you. Such is the destiny of the wicked upon the return of the Lord. [Psalm 50:16-22 NIV]*

"May God arise, may his enemies be scattered; may his foes flee before him. May you blow them away like smoke—as wax melts before the fire, may the wicked perish before God. But may the righteous be glad and rejoice before God; may they be happy and joyful. Sing to God, sing in praise of his name, extol him who rides on the clouds; rejoice before him—his name is the Lord. A father to the fatherless, a defender of widows, is God in his holy dwelling. God sets the lonely in families, he leads out the prisoners with singing; but the rebellious live in a sun-scorched land. When you, God, went out before your people, when you marched through the wilderness, the earth shook, the heavens poured down rain, before God, the One of Sinai, before God, the God of Israel. You gave abundant showers, O God; you refreshed your weary inheritance. Your people settled in it, and from your bounty, God, you provided for the poor. The Lord announces the word, and the women who proclaim it are a mighty throng: "Kings and armies flee in haste; the women at home divide the plunder. Even while you sleep among the sheep pens, the wings of my dove are sheathed with silver, its feathers with shining gold." When the Almighty scattered the kings in the land, it was like snow fallen on Mount Zalmon. Mount Bashan, majestic mountain, Mount Bashan, rugged mountain, why gaze in envy, you rugged mountain, at the mountain where God chooses to reign, where the Lord himself will dwell forever? The chariots of God are tens of thousands and thousands of thousands; the Lord has come from Sinai into his sanctuary. When you ascended on high, you took many captives; you received gifts from people, even from the rebellious — that you, Lord God, might dwell there. Praise be to the Lord, to God our Savior, who daily bears our burdens. Our God is a God who saves; from the Sovereign Lord comes escape from death. Surely God will crush the heads of his enemies, the hairy crowns of those who go on in their sins. The Lord says, "I will bring them from Bashan; I will bring them from the depths of the sea, that your feet may wade in the blood of your foes, while the tongues of your dogs have their share." Your procession, God, has come into view, the procession of my God and King into the sanctuary. In front are the singers, after them the musicians; with them are the young women playing the timbrels. Praise God in the great congregation; praise the Lord in the assembly of Israel. There is the little tribe of Benjamin, leading them, there the great throng of Judah's princes, and there the princes of Zebulun and of Naphtali. Summon your power, God; show us your

strength, our God, as you have done before. Because of your temple at Jerusalem kings will bring you gifts. Rebuke the beast among the reeds, the herd of bulls among the calves of the nations. Humbled, may the beast bring bars of silver. Scatter the nations who delight in war.

Envoys will come from Egypt; Cush will submit herself to God.

Sing to God, your kingdoms of the earth, sing praise to the Lord, to him who rides across the highest heavens, the ancient heavens, who thunders with mighty voice. Proclaim the power of God, whose majesty is over Israel, whose power is in the heavens. You, God, are awesome in your sanctuary; the God of Israel gives power and strength to his people. Praise be to God!" [Psalm 68:1-35 NIV]

The Arising: *The one who rides on the clouds would arise again, the history of Israel from their deliverance from Egypt through the wilderness by Mount Sinai into the promised land of Canaan is going to be a repeated future event in the world, where the One of Sinai is going to arise once again to deliver His people from the land of Ham, from the current corruption and bondage in this world. He would come Himself as the deliverer to deliver His people from the hand of Pharaoh by His Almighty hand to send them into the promised land of His eternal kingdom – the new heaven and earth. As the earth shook and the heavens poured down rain before God when He went out before people of Israel, when He marched through the wilderness, so also the earth would shake one more time, the heavens would pour down rain one more time and God would march His people through the earth into His kingdom one more time at the arising. [Psalm 68:4-7, Exodus 6:6 NIV]*

The Abundance: *God would give abundant showers; He would refresh His weary inheritance and settle His people settled in His kingdom, and from His bounty, He would provide for the poor. He would be a father to the fatherless, a defender of widows, in His holy dwelling, God would set the lonely in families, and lead out the prisoners with singing into prosperity; but the rebellious He would cause to live in a sun-scorched land. [Psalm 68:5-6 NIV]*

The Announcing: *The Lord would announce the word, and a mighty throng of women would proclaim it such that kings and armies would flee in haste; causing the women to divide the plunder to the extent that while the people sleep among the sheep pens, the wings of their dove, the covering that would cover them whiles they sleep would be sheathed with silver, and its feathers with shining gold; elegance and excellence would cover them in all things even in their sleep. [Psalm 68:11-13 NIV]*

The Almighty: *The Almighty would summon His power, God would show His strength, as God, as He had done before during the deliverance of Israel from Pharaoh. And as He scattered the kings in the land, such that it was like snow falling on Mount Zalmon so would it be again. With tens of thousands and thousands of thousands of chariots; the Lord would come from Sinai into His sanctuary, Zion, the majestic mountain where God has chosen to reign, where the Lord Himself would dwell forever arousing the envy gaze of Mount Bashan, the rugged mountain of many peaks. The Almighty God is a God who saves; from the Sovereign Lord comes escape from death. He would surely crush the heads of His enemies, the hairy crowns of those who go on in their sins. The Lord would bring them from Bashan; from the depths of the sea, and that His feet may wade in the blood of His foes, while the tongues of His dogs have* *their share; He would rebuke the beast among the reeds, the herd of bulls among the calves of the nations and scatter the nations who delight in war. [Psalm 68:14-16 NIV]*

The Assembly: *There would be the great congregation; the assembly of God's people in procession, the procession of God and King into His sanctuary in Jerusalem. Arrayed with singers, and musicians; with young women playing the timbrels and with a great throng of princes. The humbled, beast would bring bars of silver as gifts and envoys would come from Egypt; Cush would submit herself to God. Kingdoms of the earth, would sing praises to the Lord, to Him who rides across the highest heavens, the ancient heavens, who thunders with mighty voice, they would proclaim the power of God, whose majesty is over His people, whose power is in the heavens. God, would be awesome in His sanctuary; God would give power and strength to His people. [Psalm 68:24-26 NIV]*

Revelation;

Jesus Christ has been revealed in this last days, He is being revealed and will be revealed in the age to come. He will reveal, His power, authority, truth, kingdom, grace, glory one more time in all of the universe. To bring the final conclusion of all matters in all of history. It will be the "day of trouble", trouble for all who are not under His new covenant and in His kingdom but deliverance for all who belong to Him. [Psalm 50:1-4, Hebrews 1:2 NIV]

Removal and Renewal;

An afflicted man who had grown weak made a prayer and poured out a lament before the Lord, he said; *"In the beginning you laid the foundations of the earth, and the heavens are the work of your hands. They will perish, but you remain; they will all wear out like a garment. Like clothing you will change them and they will be discarded. But you remain the same, and your years will never end. The children of your servants will live in your presence; their descendants will be established before you."* [Psalm 102:25-28 NIV]

When the afflicted man who had grown weak poured out a lament before the Lord in prayer of a psalm, he revealed what the Lord would do to the foundations of the earth and the heavens upon the Lord's return, He will cause them to perish by wearing them out like a garment, changing and discarding them like an old clothing in order to bring about the new earth and heavens. In this new creation, the children of the Lord's servants will live in His presence and be established before Him.

A Word to God's Elect: Strangers in a strange land.

God's elects are chosen according to the foreknowledge of God the Father and through the sanctifying work of the Spirit they are brought to be obedient to Jesus Christ who are sprinkled by His blood. His election is according to His great mercy, and in His great mercy He gives new birth to His election into a living hope that is through the resurrection of Jesus Christ from the dead. His living hope gives the election an inheritance that can never perish, spoil or even fade which is kept in heaven for the elect. The faith of the elect is God's power that is shielding this inheritance until the coming of the salvation that is ready to be revealed in the last time when the Lord comes. This inheritance shielded by faith in God's power is the power that gives the election the endurance to greatly rejoice, even when for a little while they suffer grief in all kinds of trails, for the trails comes to prove the genuineness of their faith— their faith which is of greater worth than gold, gold which perishes even though refined by fire— this test of refinery of the faith of the elect is to result in praise, glory and honor when Jesus Christ is revealed. The coming salvation is a great one, therefore the elect must be alert and fully sober in their minds, setting their hope on the grace that would be brought when Jesus Christ is revealed at His coming. As obedient children they must not conform to the evil desires as of those living in ignorance of the holiness in Christ, their savior. For the one who has called them is holy and He has called them into His holiness so then, they must be holy, they are to live as foreigners here in this present world with reverent fear for the Father who judges each person's work impartially. Their big brother paid the highest price of value to ransom them, hence they must revere their value. *"For you know that it was not with perishable things such as silver or gold that you were redeemed from the empty way of life handed down to you from your ancestors, but with the precious blood of Christ, a lamb without blemish or defect. He was chosen before the creation of the world, but was revealed in these last times for your sake. Through him you believe in God, who raised him from the dead and glorified him, and so your faith and hope are in God. Now that you have purified yourselves by obeying the truth so that you have sincere love for each other, love one another deeply, from the heart. For you have been born again, not of perishable seed, but of imperishable, through the living and enduring word of God. For, "All people are like grass, and all their glory is like the flowers of the field; the grass withers and the flowers fall, but the word of the Lord endures forever." And this is the word that was preached to you." [1 Peter 1:18-25 NIV]*

The Principles-

- *The Lord will return! "Maranatha": He comes. [Psalm 18:9 NIV]*
- *The Lord will be revealed. [Psalm 68:1-2 NIV]*
- *The Lord will reward. [Psalm 18:20-24, 68:3 NIV]*
- *The Lord will resurrect. [Psalm 68:19-20 NIV]*
- *The Lord will redeem. [Psalm 18:27 NIV]*
- *The Lord will reclaim. [Psalm 68:5-6 NIV]*
- *When anyone is in Christ He goes through the cross experience, the tomb experience and the throne experience.*

- *When anyone is in Christ, all things are finished in Christ, all things are being worked in him till it's finished – tetelestai [finished] to teleios [finish].*
- *Jesus Christ descended, ascended and transcended. [Ephesians 4:10 NIV]*
- *Redemption is by God through God, with God and for God.*
- *We all have fallen short of His glory and died, He owns us so He came down to redeem us by His grace through His love for His glory.*

The Mystery of Christ – The Mystery of the Gospel:

The fruitful benefits and effects of the gospel, Jesus Christ – Christ Jesus.

The Word:

"In the beginning, the Word existed. The Word was with God, and the Word was God. He existed in the beginning with God. Through him all things were made, and apart from him nothing was made that has been made. In him was life, and that life brought light to humanity. And the light shines on in the darkness, and the darkness has never put it out. There was a man sent from God, whose name was John. He came as a witness to testify about the light, so that all might believe because of him. John was not the light, but he came to testify about the light. This was the true light that enlightens every person by his coming into the world. He was in the world, and the world was made through him. Yet the world did not recognize him. He came to his own creation, yet his own people did not receive him. However, to all who received him, those believing in his name, he gave authority to become God's children, who were born, not merely in a genetic sense, nor from lust, nor from man's desire, but from the will of God. The Word became flesh and lived among us. We gazed on his glory, the kind of glory that belongs to the Father's unique Son, who is full of grace and truth. John told the truth about him when he cried out, "This is the person about whom I said, 'The one who comes after me ranks higher than me, because he existed before me.'" We have all received one gracious gift after another from his abundance, because while the Law was given through Moses, grace and truth came through Jesus the Messiah. No one has ever seen God. The unique God, who is close to the Father's side, has revealed him." [John 1:1-18 ISV]*

The key ideas from this record by John is that;

- *The Word existed in the beginning of beginnings, not only that but the Word existed with God, and the Word that existed with God was God. He, the Word existed in the beginning with God. [John 1:1 ISV]*
- *The Word was and is EVERYTHING, since the Word is God and "Godness" means "every thingness." Let me show it this way, John's record says that "Through Him, the Word ALL THINGS were made, and apart from Him NOTHING was made that has been made." [John 1:3 ISV] For all things to be made by or through or with something, then something must be all*

things. For nothing cannot make all things or something and something can only make something but when something is all things then it can make all things. Let me put it quite simple, out of Everything comes Something, Anything and Everything; out of something comes something but not everything and out of anything comes anything but not everything. So, I put the record in a paraphrase this way; in the beginning, EVERYTHING existed. EVERYTHING was with God, and EVERYTHING was God. EVERYTHING existed in the beginning with God. Through EVERYTHING all things were made, and apart from EVERYTHING nothing was made that has been made. Better still, in the beginning, EVERBODY existed. EVERBODY was with God, and EVERYBODY was God. EVERYBODY existed in the beginning with God. Through EVERYBODY all things were made, and apart from EVERBODY nothing was made that has been made.

And remember EVERYTHING and EVERYBODY is the Word and is GOD.

- *Then obviously, In Him, the Word [everything, everybody] was life, and that life brought light to humanity. And the light shines on in the darkness, and the darkness has never put it out. Is the truth. [John 1:4-5 ISV]*
- *The Word is the true light that enlightens every person by His coming into the world. He was in the world, and the world was made through Him. [John 1:10 ISV]*
- *He, the Word of creation came to His own creation.*
- *The very creatures –people- created by the Word of creation rejected and forsook Him. [John 1:11 ISV]*
- *The creature, person or people, whoever it maybe that receives Him, that believes in His name, He gives the authority to become God's children, a child born of God's Spirit, not a child born merely in a genetic sense, or from human lust, nor from man's desire, but from the will of God.*
- *The Word became flesh, He became a human and lived among human beings, among humans on the earth. Human beings gazed on His glory, the kind of glory that belongs to the Father's unique Son, who is full of grace and truth. Whenever human beings meet the Word that became a human being they meet the fullness of glory, grace and truth. [John 1:14 ISV]*
- *John, the one who was baptizing for repentance told the truth about him when he cried out, "This is the person about whom I said, 'The one who comes after me ranks higher than me, because He existed before me.'" [John 1:30 ISV]*
- *All people who received the Word, received, are receiving and can receive one gracious gift after another from His abundance.*
- *While the Law was given through Moses, grace and truth came through Jesus the Messiah, the Word. Moses was the receiver and the giver of the Law – old covenant, the Word become flesh is the receiver and the giver of grace and truth – new covenant. [John 1:17 ISV]*

- *No one has ever seen God. The unique God, Jesus Christ who is close to the Father's side, has revealed Him. Jesus Christ is the revelation of the unseen God in the seen, He is the demonstration of the invisible God in the visible. [John 1:18 ISV]*

The Son; our example, our experience, our expression, our exaltation.

"God …has in these last days spoken to us by His Son, whom He has appointed heir of all things, and through whom He made the world. The Son is the radiance of God's glory and the exact representation of His being [person], sustaining [(up) holds] all things [everything together] by His powerful word. the Son, is appointed heir of all things, and through whom also He made the universe [worlds]. When He had by Himself purged our sins, He sat down at the right hand of the Majesty on high." [Hebrews 1:2-3 NIV, MEV]

"For those God foreknew he also predestined to be conformed to the image of his Son, that he might be the firstborn among many brothers and sisters. And those he predestined, he also called; those he called, he also justified; those he justified, he also glorified." [Romans 8:29-30 NIV]

The Son, Jesus Christ is the brightness and reflection of the glory of the Father, the exact and express likeness of the Father, the Son is the Word of creation of the worlds and the Word of sustenance of everything. The Father's desire and need is that all of His other sons conform to the image of His firstborn Son. The Son, Jesus Christ is the first fruit of all harvest of sons and the firstborn of all born sons. The Son is our example to be followed, our experience to enjoy, our expression to show, and our exaltation to esteem.

The Son of Man And Or The Son of God:

There are two distinct yet not contradictory nature of Jesus' sonship, He is the Son of Man and the Son of God. As the Son of Man, He has authority on the earth as a man and as the Son of God He has authority in heaven as God. Hence He has ultimate authority over both heaven and earth, let us explore certain scriptures that reveal the expressions of the Son.

- *A teacher of the law [a scribe] came to Jesus and said, "Teacher, I will follow you wherever you go." Jesus replied, "Foxes have dens [holes] and birds have nests, but the Son of Man has no place to lay his head [rest]." [Matthew 8:19-20 NIV, MEV]*
- *I want you [some of the scribes who said to themselves, "this fellow is blaspheming!" when Jesus said to the paralyzed man whose friends by faith brought him on a stretcher, "take heart [be courageous], son! your sins are forgiven" to know that the Son of Man has authority on earth to forgive sins. So, he said to the paralyzed man, "Get up, take your mat and go home." Then the man got up and went home. [Matthew 9:6 NIV, ISV]*

- *The Son of Man came eating and drinking, and they say, "Look, here is a glutton and a drunk [ard], a friend of tax collectors and sinners! Absolved from every act of sin, is wisdom by her kith and kin [wisdom is proved right by her deeds]." [Matthew 11:19 NIV, MEV]*

- *The Son of Man came to seek and to save the lost. [Luke 10:19 NIV]*

- *The Son of Man did not come to be served, but to serve, and to give His life as a ransom for many. [Matthew 20:28 NIV]*

- *No one has ever gone into heaven except the one who came from heaven —the Son of Man. Just as Moses lifted up the snake in the wilderness, so the Son of Man must be lifted up, that everyone who believes may have eternal life in him. [John 3:13-14 NIV]*

- *If anyone is ashamed of me and my words in this adulterous and sinful generation, the Son of Man will be ashamed of them when he comes in his Father's glory with the holy angels. I tell you, whoever publicly acknowledges me before others, the Son of Man will also acknowledge before the angels of God. But whoever disowns me before others will be disowned before the angels of God. And everyone who speaks a word against the Son of Man will be forgiven, but anyone who blasphemes against the Holy Spirit will not be forgiven. [Luke 12:8-10 NIV]*

- *He Jesus said to them, the disciples, "The Son of Man is going to be delivered [betrayed] into human hands. They will kill Him, and on the third day He will be raised to life." [Mark 9:31 NIV]*

- *The Son of Man will be delivered over to the chief priests and the teachers of the law. They will condemn Him to death and will hand Him over to the Gentiles to be mocked and flogged and crucified. On the third day he will be raised to life! [Matthew 20:18-19 NIV]*

- *As Jonah was three days and three nights in the belly of a huge fish [stomach of the sea creature], so the Son of Man will be three days and three nights in the heart of the earth. [Matthew 12:40 NIV]*

- *As you know, the Passover is two days away — and the Son of Man will be handed over to be crucified. Jesus replied, "The one who has dipped his hand into the bowl with me will betray me. The Son of Man will go just as it is written about Him. But woe to that man who betrays the Son of Man! It would be better for Him if he had not been born." Then Judas, the one who would betray Him, said, "Surely you don't mean me, Rabbi?" Jesus answered, "You have said so." He returned [after praying] to the disciples and said to them, "Are you still sleeping and resting? Look, the hour has come, and the Son of Man is delivered into the hands of sinners. Rise! Let us go! Here comes my betrayer!" The high priest said to Him, "I charge you under oath by the living God: Tell us if you are the Messiah, the Son of God." "You have said so," Jesus replied. "But I say to all of you: From now on you will see the Son of Man sitting at the right hand of the Mighty One and coming on the clouds of heaven." [Matthew 26:2, 23-25, 45-46, 62-64 NIV]*

- *At the end of the age the Son of Man will send out His angels, and they will weed out of His kingdom everything that causes sin and all who do evil [those who practice lawlessness]. They* will throw them into the blazing furnace, where there will be weeping and gnashing of teeth. Then the righteous will shine like the sun in the kingdom of their Father. Whoever has ears, let them hear. [Matthew 13:41-43 NIV]

- The Son of Man is going to come in His Father's glory with His angels, and then He will reward each person according to what they have done. "Truly I tell you, some who are standing here will not taste [experience] death before they see the Son of Man coming in His kingdom. [Matthew 16:27-28 NIV, ISV]

- Jesus said to them [the disciples after Peter answered Him, "See, we have left everything and followed You. What then shall we have?"] "Truly I tell you with certainty, at the renewal of all things [the renewed creation, the regeneration], when the Son of Man sits on His glorious throne, you who have followed me will also sit on twelve thrones, judging the twelve tribes of Israel. And everyone who has left houses or brothers or sisters or father or mother or wife or children or fields for my sake will receive a hundred times as much and will inherit eternal life. But many who are first will be last, and many who are last will be first. [Matthew 19:27-30 NIV]

- Once, on being asked by the Pharisees when the kingdom of God would come, Jesus replied, "The coming of the kingdom of God is not something that can be observed, nor will people say, 'Here it is,' or 'There it is,' because the kingdom of God is in your midst -- is within you." Then he said to his disciples, "The time is coming when you will long to see one of the days of the Son of Man, but you will not see it. People will tell you, 'There he is!' or 'Here he is!' Do not go running off after them. For the Son of Man in his day will be like the lightning, which flashes and lights up the sky from one end to the other. But first he must suffer many things and be rejected by this generation. [Luke 17:20-25 NIV]

- The Son of Man in his day will be like the lightning, which flashes and lights up the sky from one end to the other. As lightning that comes from the east is visible even in the west, so will be the coming of the Son of Man. Wherever there is a carcass, there the vultures will gather. "Immediately after the distress of those days "'the sun will be darkened, and the moon will not give its light; the stars will fall from the sky, and the heavenly bodies will be shaken.' "Then will appear the sign of the Son of Man in heaven. And then all the peoples of the earth will mourn when they see the Son of Man coming on the clouds of heaven, with power and great glory. And he will send his angels with a loud trumpet call, and they will gather his elect from the four winds, from one end of the heavens to the other. [Matthew 24:27-31 NIV]

- "When the centurion, who stood there in front of Jesus [on the cross], saw how he died, he said, "Surely this man was the Son of God!" [Mark 15:39 NIV]

The Principle:

Christ Jesus, the Son of God, the Son of Man is God and Man fully, God before all creation, in time and after time, Man in creation and in time yet since He is the only begotten Son of God by nature and not by creation, He became [also] the Son of Man by divine wisdom that He would be full of grace and truth in order to regenerate sons of man into the sons of God, bring many sons to glory. By the Spirit of holiness He was appointed the Son of God in power through His resurrection from the dead. [John 3:16, Romans 1:4, Hebrews 2:10 MEV]

The Name: the person, the power, the promise, the principle.

"In your relationships with one another, have the same mindset as Christ Jesus: Who, being in very nature God, did not consider equality with God something to be used to his own advantage; rather, he made himself nothing by taking the very nature of a servant, being made in human likeness. And being found in appearance as a man, he humbled himself by becoming obedient to death — even death on a cross! Therefore, God exalted him to the highest place and gave him the name that is above every name, that at the name of Jesus every knee should bow, in heaven and on earth and under the earth, and every tongue acknowledge that Jesus Christ is Lord, to the glory of God the Father." [Philippians 2:5-11 NIV]

The wisdom in the name is that, the name represents and reveals the persons; *nature, authority, ability, majesty, might, magnificence, excellence, exaltation, existence and essence*. The name Jesus tells of the nature of Him as the savior, His authority over everything created on earth, in heaven and beneath the earth, His ability to give and take, His majesty and magnificence as exalted in the highest place of honor in all of creation to *the right hand of the Father*. By His name Jesus in the salvation strategy of the Godhead, He became a servant man in humility onto death on the cross. He is the wisdom of God, the power of God who has become onto all of humanity; *righteousness, sanctification, redemption, glory, grace, love, power, peace, hope*. As the *person*, He is the *love* of God, as the *power*, He is the *faith* in God, as the *promise*, He is the *hope* in God and as the *principle*, He is the *mindset*, *means* of God to *majesty* in life. As the *savior*, He is the *salvation*, as the *just one*, *He* is the *justification*, as the *wise one*, He is *wisdom*.

The Principle:

- *Jesus' humility in humanity is His exaltation in name.*
- *Jesus' servant-hood in slavery is His excellency in nature.*
- *Jesus' obedience in suffering is His magnificence in maturity.*
- *The name of Jesus is the exalted name above all other names. [Philippians 2:9 NIV]*

- *At the name of Jesus, every knee bow in heaven and on earth and under the earth. [Philippians 2:10 NIV]*
- *At the name of Jesus, every tongue acknowledges that Jesus Christ is the Lord, hence glorifying the Father. [Philippians 2:11 NIV]*
- *Believe in the name of the Son of God, Jesus Christ and the power of the authority of His name.*

C: — *counsel, creation, cross, covenant, church, crown, conquest, coming*
H: — *head, heir, high priest, hope.*
R: — *rest, rock, ransom, reality, redeemer.*
I: — *image, immortal, indestructible.*
S: — *Son of God, Son of Man, Spirit of holiness, sacrifice of atonement, savior, shepherd, seed, secret.*
T: — *truth, testator, treasures.*

The Church.

The word church has moved from its meaning during the time of Jesus Christ to mean something completely different to many people. Some have the meaning to be that of a building, a structure, synagogue or sanctuary. Let's ask ourselves these questions;

- *What is the Church?*
- *What is the mandate of the Church?*
- *What is the method of the Church?*
- *What is the message of the Church?*
- *What is the might of the Church?*

Paul of Tarsus, the 1st century herald to the Gentiles for the king of the kingdom of God, Jesus Christ, presented what the Church is, its mandate, method, message, and might.

He recorded them as these:

"God placed all things under His [Jesus Christ] feet and appointed Him to be head over everything for the [good of the] church, which is His body, the fullness of Him who fills everything in every way. He is far above every ruler, authority, power, dominion, and every name that can be named [invoked], not only in the present age but also in the one to come. This grace was given me: to preach to the Gentiles the boundless riches of Christ, and to make plain to everyone the administration of this mystery, which for ages past was kept hidden in God, who created all things. His intent was that now, through the church, the manifold wisdom of God should be made known to the rulers and authorities in the heavenly realms, according to His eternal purpose that He accomplished in Christ Jesus our Lord. In Him and through faith in Him we may approach God with freedom and confidence… the Father, from whom every family in heaven and on earth derives its name. Christ is the head of the church, His body, of which He is the

Savior. Now the church submits to Christ, Christ loved the church and gave himself up for her to make her holy, cleansing her by the washing with water through the word, and to present her to himself as a radiant church, without stain or wrinkle or any other blemish, but holy and blameless. No one ever hated their own body, but they feed and care for their body, just as Christ does the church— for we are members of his body. This is a profound mystery—but I am talking about Christ and the church. God's household, which is the church of the living God, the pillar and foundation of the truth. Your bodies are temples of the Holy Spirit, who is in you, whom you have received from God, You are not your own; you were bought at a price. [Ephesians 1:22-23, 21, 3:7-12, 15, 5:23-27, 29-30, 32, 1 Timothy 3:15, 1 Corinthians 6:19-20 NIV]

From this wonderful revelation of mystery given to Paul, we can learn the true structure of the church.

The church is;

- *The Assembly of believers in Christ wherever, whenever, whoever. [Ephesians 3:7-12 NIV]*
- *The Body of Christ for functioning on the earth. [Ephesians 1:22-23 NIV]*
- *The Bride of Christ married to Him in beauty. [Ephesians 5:23-27, 29-30, 32 NIV]*
- *The Citizens of the Kingdom of God on earth and in heaven. [Ephesians 3:15 NIV]*
- *The Sanctuary and temple [individual bodies of the humans who believe in Christ] of the Spirit of God. [1 Corinthians 6:19-20 NIV]*
- *The Household and family of the living God, the family of the Father of fathers born in the newness that is in Christ and built on the pillar and foundation of the truth. [1 Timothy 3:15 NIV]*

In order for the church to fulfill its mandate of revealing, making known the manifold wisdom of God to the rulers and authorities in the heavenly realms, according to God's eternal purpose that He accomplished in Christ Jesus our Lord, the church must submit to the head, Christ Jesus. The church must submit to the washing and cleansing of Jesus Christ to become radiant and blameless without spot or wrinkle. For this reason, the head equipped the church with gifts, of which some are; *"Christ himself gave the apostles, the prophets, the evangelists, the pastors and teachers, to equip his people for works of service, so that the body of Christ may be built up until we all reach unity in the faith and in the knowledge of the Son of God and become mature, attaining to the whole measure of the fullness of Christ.*

Then we will no longer be infants, tossed back and forth by the waves, and blown here and there by every wind of teaching and by the cunning and craftiness of people in their deceitful scheming. Instead, speaking the truth in love, we will grow to become in every respect the mature body of him who is the head, that is, Christ. From him the whole body, joined and held together by every supporting ligament, grows and builds itself up in love, as each part does its work." [Ephesians 4:11-16 NIV]

From the passage in Ephesians, Christ gifts the church, persons of *apostles, prophets, evangelists, pastors, and teachers* who are for the *equipping* of His body for *works of service*, nothing more, nothing else. The gifts are for *building up* the body of Christ, for *maturing* the body from infancy until all reach *unity in the faith* and in the *knowledge of the Son of God* and thus *reconciling the world* to God through Christ. *[Ephesians 4:11-13 NIV].* The gifts to the church are to bring people to the person of Christ, to the kingdom of Christ not to a physical building, religion of rites and rituals or the gifts themselves.

The Church and The Armor of God:

"Finally, be strong in the Lord, relying on his mighty strength. Put on the whole armor of God so that you may be able to stand firm against the devil's strategies. For our struggle is not against human opponents, but against rulers, authorities, cosmic powers in the darkness around us, and evil spiritual forces in the heavenly realm. For this reason, take up the whole armor of God so that you may be able to take a stand whenever evil comes. And when you have done everything you could, you will be able to stand firm. Stand firm, therefore, having fastened the belt of truth around your waist, and having put on the breastplate of righteousness, and being firm-footed in the gospel of peace. In addition to having clothed yourselves with these things, having taken up the shield of faith, with which you will be able to put out all the flaming arrows of the evil one, also take the helmet of salvation and the sword of the Spirit, which is the word of God. Pray in the Spirit at all times with every kind of prayer and request. Likewise, be alert with your most diligent efforts and pray for all the saints. Pray also for me, so that, when I begin to speak, the right words will come to me. Then I will boldly make known the secret of the gospel, for whose sake I am an ambassador in chains, desiring to declare the gospel as boldly as I should." *"We are living in the world, but we do not wage war in a world-like way (how does the world wage war). For the weapons of our warfare (what are these weapons) are not those of the world. Instead, they have the power of God to demolish fortresses; stronghold. We tear down arguments and every proud obstacle; pretension that is raised against the knowledge of God, we taking every thought captive in order to obey the Messiah. Once your obedience is complete, we will be ready to reprimand every type of disobedience."* *[Ephesians 6:10-20, 2 Corinthians 10:3-6 NIV]*

Action determines Reaction and Attack determines Defense.

The principle of action and reaction as well as attack and defense is fundamental in nature, it is a universal law set up by the Creator. Man uses this law in all fields and endeavors, the area of science, sport, soldiering and many more, the defense of an army must be modeled to effectively and efficiently counteract and overcome the attack of the opposition. The defense of an attorney of law must be strategic enough to cancel out the case of the accusing counselor for justice and probity to be met in the law court. If these principles hold true, then the armor one wears can reveal the attack one can expect to be under.

There is a fight we fighting and, in this fight, though we are in the body and of blood, in this seen and visible realm it is not a fight in the seen and visible realm. It is not a fight with guns, drones and jets, but it is a fight in the unseen invisible realm against principalities, against powers, against the rulers of the darkness of this world, and against spiritual forces of evil in the heavenly places. The weapons we fight with are not the weapons of the world, on the contrary, they have divine power to demolish strongholds, demolish arguments, imaginations and every high pretension thing that sets itself up against the knowledge of God, and taking captive every thought to make it obedient to Christ. The weapons are the armor of God, being mighty through God Himself, so we must be strong in the Lord and in the power of His might. Paul of Tarsus, the servant of Jesus Christ gave the analogy of this epic battle of the world between the people of the Way, using the life of solider in battle in the Roman world. In the analogy, he compares this struggle and conflict of contention and confrontation in life with principal entities, rulers, authorities, cosmic powers in the darkness around, and evil spiritual forces in the heavenly realm to wearing the armor of a solider and named it the "armor of God". Take up the whole armor of God that we will be able to resist in the evil day, and having done all, to stand. We must stand having our waist girded with truth, having put on the breastplate of righteousness, having our feet fitted with the readiness of the gospel of peace, and above all, taking the shield of faith, with which we will be able to extinguish all the fiery arrows of the evil one. We take the helmet of salvation and the sword of the Spirit, which is the word of God. We pray in the Spirit always with all kinds of prayer and supplication. We are to be alert with all perseverance and supplication.

The Belt of Truth [Ephesians 6:14 NIV]:

Truth bonds and binds, it does not divide, in order to wear the belt of truth it supposes that the adversary attacks with lies and falsehood. Your defense as a person in Christ is to know the truth that sets free, Jesus Christ His Kingdom and Righteousness in the new covenant and stand with it as against the false arguments of the adversary.

The Breastplate of Righteousness [Ephesians 6:14 NIV]: for one to put on the breastplate of righteousness, it stands to reason that the enemy attacks with acts of unrighteousness. The righteousness of those who are strong in the Lord is from and by believing in Christ Jesus as the apostle and High Priest of our confession and as the perfect Lamb of God that has taken away the sin of the world.

The Gospel of Peace [Ephesians 6:15 NIV]: in this battle the foundation and root must be firm, if the foundation and root are not on a firm ground, one will fall, and this firm -- footed foundation is the gospel of peace; the good news that through Jesus Christ humanity has access to the Father in freedom and confidence and there is no enmity between God and man such that man can and must come to the Father yet the opposition, the foes, forces will oppose with news of chaos, condemnation, accusation, bad news of enmity between God and man.

The Shield of Faith [Ephesians 6:16 NIV]: shield protects against the fiery arrows of the enemy; this shield of faith extinguishes and puts out all the flaming arrows of the evil one. The flaming arrows of the evil one is fear, unbelief, misbelief and doubt in the authenticity, originality and uniqueness of the Father, Son and Spirit, fighting against your belief in His nature and essence. Fight the good fight of faith, keep holding on to your faith in the Lord with your shield, for through your faith you are shielded by God's power until the coming of the salvation in our Lord Jesus Christ which would be revealed in the last time together with the inheritance that can never perish, spoil or fade but kept in heaven for you as a result of the living hope through the resurrection of Jesus Christ from the dead.

The Helmet of Salvation [Ephesians 6:17 NIV]: the thief attacks salvation to steal it. Salvation is the grace offered by the free gift of God to redeem humanity from all wickedness and to purify for Himself a people that are His very own, eager to do what is good. The thief wants to steal, kill and destroy the gift of redemption.

The Sword of the Spirit; Word of God [Ephesians 6:17 NIV]: without the sword one cannot mount an attack, but with the sword of the Spirit you can attack the enemy, one cannot make an offensive move without the sword of the Spirit, the Word of God. The word [Jesus Christ] revealed in the heart is the sword of the Spirit. The scriptures [written word], reveals Jesus Christ. Jesus, the Word made flesh has overcome so too is he who uses the sword of the Spirit.

Armor Applied [Ephesians 6:18 NIV]:

Know the truth and be set free, live the righteous life and be secured, fight the good fight of faith and win the crown of glory, be reconciled to God, obtain salvation in Christ, live and walk in the Spirit always, let the Word of God dwell in you richly at all times, pray in the Spirit with all kinds of prayers and be an overcomer in the Lord as one who stands firm even when the evil day comes. With this armory we are able to demolish fortresses, strongholds of falsehood. We tear down arguments that are hollow and deceptive and every proud obstacle that is a pretension of human philosophy and tradition which is raised against the knowledge of God, we take every thought captive in order to obey the wisdom and power found in Christ.

Word to the Church: The Ministry and Message of Reconciliation.

The church must be the vehicle for transporting the world back to God. Carrying with it the message of reconciliation, repentance for the forgiveness of sins in the name of Jesus Christ to all the nations. Under the power of the Spirit, we must send the kingdom of God and His righteousness in Christ Jesus' new covenant to all nations, tribe, people, arena and corridor of life. As the Messiah has suffered and been raised up from the dead on the third day, we must proclaim in His name the repentance and forgiveness of sin by His suffering and successes, being clothed with power from on high. We must be compelled by Christ's love, being convinced that one died for all and therefore all died, that the one died for all so that all who live must no longer live for themselves but for the one who died for them all and was raised again for them all. We must partner God in reconciling the world to Himself in Christ as He is not counting people's sins against them for it has been counted against Christ on the cross. We must work as ambassadors of Christ committed with the ministry of reconciliation and the message of reconciliation.

The Principles;

- *We need men of the Kingdom of God and new covenant's Righteousness, with the message of the Kingdom of God and new covenant's Righteousness, bearing the marks of the Kingdom of God and new covenant's Righteousness.*
- *The derivatives of the Godhead; love, faithfulness, justice, righteousness, peace… do not deviate or change [increase or decrease], they are a constant.*
- *Without Christ there is no Church of Christ.*
- *Christian and or Church is the picture of who Christ is to the world.*
- *God is appealing to, pleading with and imploring the world, specifically and especially you, to be reconciled to Him through Christ. Because He made Christ who was sinless and had no experience with sin to experience sin and become a sin offering for you.*
- *In Him, Jesus Christ we Be-Come God's righteousness, not my own righteousness nor the laws righteousness. [Romans 3:21-26, 2 Corinthians 5:21 NIV]*

C: — Christ.
H: — household – home of the living loving Godhead.
U: — universal unit, united diversity of every tribe, ethnic, nation in heaven and on earth.
R: — radiant, righteous, reign, realm.
C: — covenant, creation, counsel, city.
H: — "hospital", heritage – heirs.

S: — seal, sanctifier, Spirit of; God, Christ, glory.

P: — promise, power, presence.

I: — instructor.

R: — revealer, reign, realm, river of living waters.

I: — intercessor.

T: — testifier [of], truth, transformer.

C: -- comforter, counsellor.

H: -- helper.

A: -- advocate, advisor, anointing.

T: -- teacher, trainer, testator.

New Covenant:

The one who believes in Jesus Christ, enters into His new covenant, that everlasting covenant that He established by His blood and death. What is a covenant? A covenant is a counsel of accord and agreement based on an oath with ordinances, offerings, obligations and objectives for engagement, entered into between two or more authors with vouchers for validation or nullification based on testimony of the testator[s]. There are various requirements of or for a covenant such as; partners, promises, penalties, testator, witness, mediator, guarantor, offering, oath and seal.

"While they were eating, Jesus took bread, and when he had given thanks, he broke it and gave it to his disciples, saying, "Take and eat; this is my body (broken and given for you)." Then he took a cup, and when he had given thanks, he gave it to them, saying, "Drink from it, all of you. This is my blood of the new covenant, which is poured out for many for the forgiveness of sins." [Luke 22:17-20 NIV]

It is the new covenant of the Spirit, with Christ as the mediator and the Spirit of Christ as the minister. It is the glorious covenant, whiles the old covenant had glory, and its glory cannot be compared to that of the new covenant. The old covenant which is the covenant of law initiated at Mount Sinai through Moses with the Israelites 430 years after God's covenant and its promises to Abraham. A covenant that brought death, condemnation and was engraved in letters on stone, such that the Israelites could not look steadily at its glory, the glory on the face of its mediator, Moses even though its glory was transitory. But the ministry of the Spirit, the new covenant is even more glorious, it is the ministry that brings life and righteousness! With surpassing and lasting glory! Jesus Christ is the guarantor of the new superior better eternal covenant with its promises and inheritance. And since Jesus lives forever, His covenant is also forever. Paul of Tarsus was specifically appointed as a herald, an apostle and a faithful teacher of this new covenant for the Gentiles.

"There is one God. There is also one mediator between God and human beings - a human, the Messiah Jesus. He gave himself as a ransom for everyone, the testimony at the proper time." "For there is one God and one mediator between God and mankind, the man Christ Jesus, who gave himself as a ransom for all people. This has now been witnessed to at the proper time."[1 Timothy 2:5-7 ISV, NIV]

The writer of Hebrews weaves the beauty of the new covenant through Jesus Christ using the life example of the ancient Hebrews in his writing to the Hebrews. He asserted the superiority of Jesus as a Son of Man over the angles, and as a faithful Son in the father's household over the faithful servant Moses. He then turns to the superiority of Jesus' ministry as a high priest of the new covenant as against that of the Levitical priesthood and how the new covenant is better, eternal, greater and powerful than the old covenant.

Jesus by the new covenant is superior to the angles in His; name, son ship, worship, kingship and recreation power. Jesus has inherited the name that is better than angels, a name He declares to His brothers in the congregation – all who are under the new covenant. He has being appointed as the firstborn son forever and forever, He has inherited a kingdom of righteousness by which He reign over all, in heaven and on earth, even beneath. All creation worship Him and He holds the power to recreate the entire universe through the power of the new covenant in Him through which He has become the source of salvation for all.

In superiority to Moses, whereas Moses could not give eternal rest to the people that he delivered from Egypt into the Promised Land, Jesus Christ has the power to give eternal rest for all who come to Him under the new covenant.

In superiority of priesthood, Jesus' priesthood is completely different and greater than that of the house of Levi, His is eternal, indestructible, perfect, effective, and strong and mighty, even His laws are different. *"Now if perfection could have been attained through the Levitical priesthood—for on this basis the people received the Law—what further need would there be to speak of appointing another kind of priest according to the order of Melchizedek, not one according to the order of Aaron? When a change in the priesthood takes place, there must also be a change in the Law. Indeed, because it was weak and ineffective, the former commandment has been annulled, 19 since the Law made nothing perfect, and a better hope is presented, by which we approach God."* [Hebrews 7:11-12, 18 NIV]

Jesus' priesthood is superior because it was based on an oath, and also perpetual since He lives forever whereas others were without an oath and as mortal men were subject to death; *"None of this happened without an oath. Others became priests without any oath, but Jesus became a priest with an oath [Psalm 110:4] In this way, Jesus has become the guarantor of a better covenant. There have been many priests, since each one of them had to stop serving in office when he died. But because Jesus lives forever, he has a permanent priesthood. Therefore, because he always lives to intercede for them, he is able to save completely those who come to God through him."* [Hebrews 7:20-25 NIV]

This is the sort of covenant and priesthood every human being needs, one who is holy, innocent, pure, set apart from sinners, and exalted above the heavens. One who does not and has no need to offer sacrifices every day like human earthly *high priests* do, first for his own sins and then for those of the people, because He has done so once for all when He sacrificed Himself. The Law - all resemblance of religion- appoints as high priests men who are weak, but the promised oath, which came after the Law, resulted in the Son who is eternally perfect.

"Jesus has now obtained a more superior ministry, since the covenant he mediates is founded on better promises. For if the first covenant had been faultless, there would have been no need to look for a second one. But God found something wrong with his people when he said, "Look! The days are coming, declares the Lord, when I will establish a new covenant with the house of Israel and with the house of Judah. It will not be like the covenant that I made with their ancestors at the time when I took them by the hand and brought them out of the land of Egypt. Because they did not remain loyal to my covenant, I ignored them, declares the Lord. For this is the covenant that I will make with the house of Israel after that time, declares the Lord: I will put my laws in their minds and write them on their hearts. I will be their God, and they will be my people. Never again will everyone teach his neighbor or his brother by saying, 'Know the Lord,' because all of them will know me, from the least important to the most important. For I will be merciful regarding their wrong deeds, and I will never again remember their sins." In speaking of a "new" covenant, he has made the first one obsolete, and what is obsolete and aging will soon disappear." [Hebrews 8:7-13 NIV]

The old covenant was faulty and there was *"something"* wrong with the covenant, so God declared to them that a time would come when He would establish a *"new covenant"*, this new covenant is not *"like"* the old covenant that was made between the ancestors of Israel when the Lord took them by the hand through the hands of Moses, Aaron and Miriam and brought them out of the land of Egypt.*[Hebrews 8:8-9 NIV]* Disloyalty to the covenant was a major issue and obeying the laws of the covenant was impossible because of the *"heart of stone"* hence for this new covenant the heart of stone must be removed and replaced with the *"heart of flesh"* as stated *''I will give you a new heart and put a new spirit in you; I will remove from you your of heart of stone and give you a heart of flesh''* [Ezekiel 36:26 NIV] so that the laws can be put in the minds and be written on hearts. Knowing the Lord would come from within, inside not from without, outside, it would be internal not external and there would be mercy concerning wrong deeds and no remembrance of sins, for the old covenant is obsolete and aging to soon disappear.

Therefore, when time for the new covenant to be established came, its high priest, Jesus the Messiah went through the greater and more perfect tabernacle not made by human hands and not part of this creation, this physical world to offer blood but not the blood of animals like goats, calves or others but by His own blood, He entered the *"Holy of Holies"* only once and for all to secure the *"eternal redemption"* of humanity. His blood of the new covenant is powerful and efficacious as He offered Himself unblemished to God through the eternal Spirit to cleanse our consciences from dead actions so we can serve the living God. *"This is why the Messiah is the mediator of a new covenant; so that those who are called may receive the eternal inheritance promised them, since a death has occurred that redeems them from the offenses committed under the first covenant. For where there is a will, the death of the one who made it must be established. For a will is in force only when somebody has died, since it never takes effect as long as the one who made it is alive."* [Hebrews 9:15-17 NIV]

Christ went into the true sanctuary in heaven itself to appear now in God's presence on behalf of every human being, He did not go there to sacrifice Himself again and again if that was so He would have had to suffer repeatedly since the creation of the world but He at the end of the ages appeared once for all to remove sin by His sacrifice and would appear a second time to bring salvation to all who eagerly awaits Him but not to deal with sin but to judge as appointed.

As a matter of fact, all the people of old, the heroes of the hall of faith; Abraham, Sarah, Isaac… were all looking and waiting for the new covenant in Christ Jesus. *"All these people [Gideon, Moses, Rehab, Daniel,] won approval for their faith but they did not receive what was promised, since God had planned something better for us, so that they would not be perfected without us." [Hebrews 11:39-40 NIV]* The fathers of faith were only made perfect together with those who live under the new covenant in Christ Jesus.

The Covenant Keeping God; A word to the covenant people.

There is an aspect of the living God which is so profound, that is, when He takes an oath of covenant, He fulfills it, by virtue of His Holiness and Faithfulness, there is no oath of covenant that He swears by and does not fulfill even for thousands of thousands of generations. It was based on His same oath that He fulfilled the new covenant in His Son, God will remember His new covenant in Christ with the people under this covenant, so the scriptures say; *"God has said, "I will never leave you or abandon you." Hence, we can confidently say, "The Lord is my helper; I will not be afraid. What can anyone do to me?" [Hebrews 13:6, Psalm 118:6, 7 NIV]* The almighty God by His word will never leave or abandon the people of His covenant, let us have the same spirit of faith as the psalmist and declare confidently that He, the Lord is our helper hence we will not be afraid of anyone nor anything. Jesus, the Messiah, who is the same yesterday and today- and forever! Will keep His covenant promises and fulfill them. Let us endure as He even endured the insults of men whiles looking forward to the permanent city that is coming at His coming. For we have an advocate with the Father, Jesus Christ, the Righteous One who is our Mediator, the Way, the Truth and the Life and by whose atoning sacrifice our sins are forgiven. *"Now may the God of peace, who by the blood of the eternal covenant brought back from the dead our Lord Jesus, the Great Shepherd of the sheep, equip you with everything good to do his will, accomplishing in us what pleases him through Jesus, the Messiah. To him be glory forever and ever! Amen." [Hebrews 13:20-21 NIV]*

The Pillars of the New Covenant;

- Partners: *The new covenant is the partnership between the only one God, the only one mediator man – Jesus Christ and all of mankind.*

- Promises: *The promises of the new covenant are eternal, eternal salvation, eternal life, better hope, and better things.*
- Penalties: *The penalty of the new covenant is that without faith in the graciousness of Jesus Christ one is lost and dead forever. Without Christ Jesus, one is nullified from the covenant of promise.*
- Testator -- Witness – Mediator – Guarantor -- Advocate: *The Father, Son and Spirit makes up the testator, mediator and guarantor of the covenant.*
- Offering: *Christ Jesus is the offering of the covenant.*
- Oath: *God took an oath by Himself to fulfill the covenant by Himself with man.*
- Seal: *The Spirit of God is the seal of the covenant.*

C: — Christ, cross, church, creation, counsel.

O: — oath, offering, obedience, ordinance, obligation, objectives.

V: — vow, voucher, validator.

E: — engagements, entrance, experiences.

N: — name.

A: — author, accord, agreement.

N: — nullification.

T: — testator, testifier, testimony.

New Creation:

Jesus is the author and pioneer of a totally new order. He takes away the old and completely creates the new. The old creation is removed and replaced with the new creation. A creation that is built from ground up, from the concept level to the design level to the production or manufacturing level. The new creation is made up of the new man, new humanity, the new life, the new city, new song, new law; heaven and earth. The faithful teacher to the Gentiles said this; *"May I never boast except in the cross of our Lord Jesus Christ, through which the world has been crucified to me, and I to the world. Neither circumcision nor uncircumcision means anything; what counts is the new creation." [Galatians 6:14-15 NIV]* What really matter in life on earth? It is often said that the two greatest days in the life of a man are the day one was born and the day one finds out why one was born, but I stand to say that the third day is the most important of all the days, the day that a person believes Jesus Christ and receives the Spirit of Christ, it is this day that makes the ultimate change in the destiny of a man, it is the day a man becomes the *"new creation"* which is what counts and means everything. The boast of the human race must be that by the power of the cross of Christ Jesus the Lord, the world has been crucified to us and us to the world and that whether *"circumcision nor uncircumcision"* we are a new creation; *[Galatians 6:15 NIV] "For Christ's love compels us, because we are convinced that one died for all, and therefore all died. And he died for all, that those who live should no longer live for themselves but for him who died for them and was raised again. So from now on we regard no one from a worldly point of view. Though we once regarded Christ in this way, we do so no longer. Therefore, if anyone is in Christ, the new creation has come: The old has gone, the new is here!" [2 Corinthians 5:14-17 NIV]*

The new creation is the result of Jesus' death on the cross and resurrection from the dead, by His dead and resurrection He brought about the new creation for all of mankind.

New Humanity:

In Christ, the new creation has come: the old has gone, the new is here! The new that has come or is here brings about the new man and humanity. Humanity although came from one man, became divided as time went by, but God by election chose Abraham that through his seed he would make him a great nation and other nations will be blessed through him. The nations of the world were now divided into the "people of God", Israel and the "Gentiles". But in Christ He has made one nation out of the two as it was originally so by means of His death on the cross. The new humanity is the handiwork of God, it is God craftsmanship and workmanship of creation in Christ in order that this new humanity would *"perform good works"* that God Himself *"prepared in advance for us to do" [Ephesians 2:10 NIV]*

Formerly all who were Gentiles by birth and were called *"uncircumcised"* by the Israelites who called themselves the *"circumcision" [which is done in the body by human hands.] [Ephesians 2:11 NIV]* This issue of circumcision and uncircumcision made the Gentiles to be separated from Christ, being *"excluded from citizenship in Israel and foreigners to the covenants of the promise, without hope and without God in the world." [Ephesians 2: 11-12 NIV]* But through Christ Jesus something has happened in order that the Gentiles who were far off and away have been brought near and into citizenship and partakers of the covenants of the promise, that which happened is that Jesus Christ by His blood on the cross has become the peace of all mankind, *"He Himself is our peace",* By the blood on the cross *"He has made the two groups one and has destroyed the barrier, the dividing wall of hostility, by setting aside in his flesh the law with its commands and regulations. His purpose was to create in himself one new humanity out of the two, thus making peace, and in one body to reconcile both of them to God through the cross, by which he put to death their hostility. He came and preached peace to you who were far away and peace to those who were near. For through him we both have access to the Father by one Spirit. Consequently, you are no longer foreigners and strangers, but fellow citizens with God's people and also members of his household, built on the foundation of the apostles and prophets, with Christ Jesus himself as the chief cornerstone. In him the whole building is joined together and rises to become a holy temple in the Lord. And in him you too are being built together to become a dwelling in which God lives by his Spirit." [Ephesians 2:14-22 NIV]*

New Man Nature:

Under the new creation, there is the new man. The new man who is created in the image of its Creator and after the likeness of its creator. Even though at present, the new man lives in the body of the old man, it must have the new attitude of mind of the new man, and must put off the old self but rather put on the new self. The new self is made new in the attitude of mind by being renewed in knowledge in the image of its Creator. Every human being born into this world has the old nature from the old man inherited from the first Adam, and everyone who believes Christ and receives the Spirit of Christ inherits the new nature from the new man, which must be expressed in life and living. The new man with the new nature must no longer live in the old nature with the futility of thinking, with the darkened understanding that separates a man from God due to ignorance from a hardened heart. Such a heart has lost all sensitivity hence it gives oneself over to sensuality, where by one indulges in every kind of impurity whiles being full of greed.

"That however, is not the way of life you learned when you heard about Christ and were taught in him in accordance with the truth that is in Jesus. You were taught, with regard to your former way of life, to put off your old self, which is being corrupted by its deceitful desires; to be made new in the attitude of your minds; and to put on the new self, created to be like God in true righteousness and holiness." [Ephesians 4:20-24 NIV]

The truth in Jesus is that one in Christ must *"put off the old self"*, [Ephesians 4:22 NIV] that self which is corrupted by deceitful desires and one must *"put on the new self"* [Ephesians 4:24 NIV] and be made new in the minds attitude, this new self is created to be like God in true righteousness and holiness. This is so because the person who belongs to Christ has been raised with Christ since we died and were raised with Him, we must set the heart on *"things above"* [Colossians 3:1-2 NIV] where Christ is, the exalted place of excellence at the right hand of God. The mind of the new man must be set on the things above not on *"earthly things"* [Colossians 3:2 NIV]. The life of the new man is now hidden with Christ in God, Christ is the life of the new man now such that when, Christ appears the new man would appear with Him in glory. The new man is therefore supposed to *"put to death"* [Colossians 3:5 NIV] everything that belongs to the earthly old man nature; *"sexual immorality, impurity, lust, evil desires and greed, which is idolatry. Because of these, the wrath of God is coming. You used to walk in these ways, in the life you once lived. But now you must also rid yourselves of all such things as these: anger, rage, malice, slander, and filthy language from your lips. Do not lie to each other, since you have taken off your old self with its practices and have put on the new self, which is being renewed in knowledge in the image of its Creator.... Therefore, as God's chosen people, holy and dearly loved, clothe yourselves with compassion, kindness, humility, gentleness and patience. Bear with each other and forgive one another if any of you has a grievance against someone. Forgive as the Lord forgave you. And over all these virtues put on love, which binds them all together in perfect unity."* [Colossians 3:5-14 NIV] All these are happening because in Christ there is a circumcision performed by the Spirit not by human hands, which puts off our whole self-ruled by the flesh. Our deadness in sin has been buried with baptism into Christ and resurrected into life of righteousness and the uncircumcision of our flesh has been circumcised bring us into fullness. *[See Colossians 2:10-14 NIV]*

New Life:

The powerless old life is also taken away and a new life of power is brought in. *"His divine power has given us everything we need for a godly life through our knowledge of him who called us by his own glory and goodness. Through these he has given us his very great and precious promises, so that through them you may participate in the divine nature, having escaped the corruption in the world caused by evil desires." [2 Peter 1:2-4 NIV]*

The divine power of the Father and the Son has given us in Christ, everything that we need for a godly life now, this is through our knowledge of God and our Lord Christ Jesus, our knowledge of His calling by His own glory and goodness, a calling into His very great and precious promises that we may participate in His divine nature, thereby we would escape the corruption in the world caused by evil desires. The new life of those who belong to Christ is that, by His divine power and divine nature we must live a godly life in our calling in Christ as we grow in our knowledge of Him. As a result of this new life we must make every effort to add to our faith, goodness, knowledge, self-control, perseverance, godliness, mutual affection and love for possessing such qualities in increasing measure makes our lives effective and productive in our knowledge of our Lord Jesus Christ.

Everything that happened to Christ on the cross, in the grave and on the throne, happened *for* you, happened *with* you and happened *to* you. We were buried with Him through *"baptism into death"*, we were raised with Him from the dead through *"the glory of the Father"* in order that we would live a new life in Him and through Him. *[Romans 6:4 NIV]*

"We were therefore buried with him through baptism into death in order that, just as Christ was raised from the dead through the glory of the Father, we too may live a new life. For if we have been united with him in a death like his, we will certainly also be united with him in a resurrection like his. For we know that our old self was crucified with him so that the body ruled by sin might be done away with, that we should no longer be slaves to sin — because anyone who has died has been set free from sin. Now if we died with Christ, we believe that we will also live with him. For we know that since Christ was raised from the dead, he cannot die again; death no longer has mastery over him. The death he died, he died to sin once for all; but the life he lives, he lives to God."[Romans 6:4-11 NIV]

By our death, burial and resurrection with Christ, our old self was crucified in the death and burial and our new self was resurrected in the rising in order that we would live a new life to God, a life in which sin has no mastery over because we have been set free from the slavery of sin. We have become alive to God in Christ Jesus hence we must not let sin reign in our mortal body so as to obey its evil desires, we must not allow our parts to sin as *"instrument of wickedness"* [Romans

6:13 NIV] and *"slaves to sin"* *[Romans 6:6 NIV]* instead we must offer the parts of ourselves as *"instrument of righteousness"* *[Romans 6:13 NIV]* and *"slaves of righteousness"* *[Romans 6:18 NIV]* to God in regard as one brought from death to life by the grace of God. *"For sin shall no longer be your master, because you are not under the law, but under grace."* *[Romans 6:14 NIV]*

New Law:

"A new command I [Jesus] give you: Love one another. As I have loved you, so you must love one another. By this everyone will know that you are my disciples, if you love one another." *[John 13:34-35 NIV]*

Under the newness in Christ, we do as Christ has done for and to us, we love as He has loved us, we give as He has given to us, and we forgive as He has forgiven us. His love is by and from His Spirit which He has poured out inside, without the Spirit of love we cannot love as Christ loved and loves. *"Let us continuously love one another, because love comes from God. Everyone who loves has been born from God and knows God. The person who does not love does not know God, because God is love. This is how God's love was revealed among us: God sent his uniquely existing Son into the world so that we might live through him. This is love: not that we have loved God, but that he loved us and sent his Son to be the atoning sacrifice for our sins. Dear friends, if this is the way God loved us, we must also love one another. No one has ever seen God. If we love one another, God lives in us, and his love is perfected in us. This is how we know that we abide in him and he in us: he has given us his Spirit. We have seen for ourselves and can testify that the Father has sent his Son to be the Savior of the world. God abides in the one who acknowledges that Jesus is the Son of God, and he abides in God. We have come to know and rely on the love that God has for us. God is love, and the person who abides in love abides in God, and God abides in him. This is how love has been perfected among us: we will have confidence on the Day of Judgment because, during our time in this world, we are just like him. There is no fear where love exists. Rather, perfect love banishes fear, for fear involves punishment, and the person who lives in fear has not been perfected in love. We love because God first loved us. Whoever says, "I love God," but hates his brother is a liar. The one who does not love his brother whom he has seen cannot love the God whom he has not seen. And this is the commandment that we have from him: the person who loves God must also love his brother. [1John 4:7-21 NIV]* God is the *first lover*, He first loved the world and showed His love by sending His only *Beloved* Son to be the savior of the world by atoning for our sins in order that we would live through Him. And because He expects us to love one another as He has loved us, He sent the Spirit of love into our hearts to enable us love one another. We must continually love with the love that comes from God, who is love. Love and fear do not coexist neither can one love God and not love the fellow man, for the person who abides in love by the Spirit of love, abides in God and relies on the love of God.

New Body: *The Tents, The Temple of God: Earthly & Heavenly.*

"For we know that if the earthly tent we live in is destroyed, we have a building from God, an eternal house in heaven, not built by human hands. Meanwhile we groan, longing to be clothed instead with our heavenly dwelling, because when we are clothed, we will not be found naked. For while we are in this tent, we groan and are burdened, because we do not wish to be unclothed but to be clothed instead with our heavenly dwelling, so that what is mortal may be swallowed up by life. Now the one who has fashioned us for this very purpose is God, who has given us the Spirit as a deposit, guaranteeing what is to come."[2 Corinthians 5:1-5 NIV] It is of a truth that everyone born into this world would one day die, the physical body, our *"earthly tent or house" [2 Corinthians 5:1 NIV]* one day would be destroyed by death. But the deposit of guarantee by the Spirit for those who belong to Christ is that, they have a *"building from God" [2 Corinthians 5:1 NIV]*, this building is an *"eternal house in heaven"* a *"heavenly dwelling" [2 Corinthians 5:1 NIV]* not built by human hands but fashioned purposely by God. It is only when one who is in Christ is unclothed of the earthly dwelling, can one be clothed with the heavenly dwelling. For we must be clothed with the heavenly dwelling, but we must be *unclothed to be clothed*, and when this happens, the mortal man would be swallowed up by life and not be found naked.

The question that usually comes to mind about the new body is; *"How are the dead raised? With what kind of body will they come?" [1 Corinthians 15:35 NIV]* An analogue that was used to illustrate the answer for such question was given by Paul the servant of Christ; *"What you sow does not come to life unless it dies. When you sow, you do not plant the body that will be, but just a seed, perhaps of wheat or of something else. But God gives it a body as he has determined, and to each kind of seed he gives its own body." [1 Corinthians 15:36-38 NIV]* The illustration he used was from the agro-culture, in the world of farming, when one sows a seed of any kind, the seed must die first in order to come to life again, the dying of the seed is the death of the human body and the coming to life of the seed is the resurrection of the body, again the body of the seed that comes to life is not the same body of the seed that was sown and died. The new seed that comes to life is given a new body as determined by God and to every kind of seed, its new body is according to its kind of body. So also the new body would be determined by God according to the kind of body that was sown; *"Not all flesh is the same: People have one kind of flesh, animals have another, birds another and fish another. There are also heavenly bodies and there are earthly bodies; but the splendor of the heavenly bodies is one kind, and the splendor of the earthly bodies is another. The sun has one kind of splendor, the moon another and the stars another; and star differs from star in splendor. So, will it be with the resurrection of the dead. The body that is sown is perishable, it is raised imperishable; it is sown in dishonor, it is raised in glory; it is sown in weakness, it is raised in power; it is sown a natural body, it is raised a spiritual body. If there is a natural body, there is also a spiritual body. So, it is written: "The first man Adam became a living being"; the last Adam, a life-giving spirit. The spiritual did not come first, but the natural, and after that the spiritual. The first man was of the dust of the earth; the second man is of heaven. As was the earthly man, so are those who are of the earth; and as is the heavenly man, so also are those who are of heaven. And just as we have borne the image of the earthly man, so shall we bear the image of the heavenly man." [1 Corinthians 15:39-49 NIV]*

Those in the *"first Adam, the earthly man"* [1 Corinthians 45 NIV] have the earthly man's tent, the body type of Adam and his image, and those in the *"last Adam, the heavenly man"* [1 Corinthians 15:46 NIV] at the resurrection would have the heavenly man's tent, the body type of Christ and his image. They would sow the body of the earthy man at death and reap the body of the heavenly man at the resurrection, the body of the earthly man is *perishable*, is in *dishonor*, is in *weakness* and is *natural* but as it is sown at dead in these states, it would be raised; *imperishable*, in *glory*, in *power* and *spiritual* at the resurrection. *[1 Corinthians 15:42-44 NIV]* Every human presently bears the image of the earthly man-- from *the dust of the earth* but at the resurrection, those in Christ would bear the image of the heavenly man – from *heaven [1 Corinthians 15:47-48 NIV]*. Inheriting the kingdom of God is not by *flesh and blood* nor does the *perishable* inherit the *imperishable*. *[1 Corinthians 15:50 NIV]* The kingdom of God is imperishable hence perishable bodies of flesh and blood cannot inherit it except the imperishable bodies of the spirit. *"For the perishable must clothe itself with the imperishable, and the mortal with immortality. When the perishable has been clothed with the imperishable, and the mortal with immortality, then the saying that is written will come true: "Death has been swallowed up in victory."*

"Where, O death, is your victory?

Where, O death, is your sting?"

The sting of death is sin, and the power of sin is the law. But thanks be to God! He gives us the victory through our Lord Jesus Christ." [1 Corinthians 15:53-58 NIV] By the victory of our Lord Jesus Christ over death, sin and the law, our decaying bodies would be clothed with un-decaying bodies in Him, our mortality would be clothed with immortality through His immortality.

New Heaven and Earth, City -- Country:

The present heaven and earth are not the final destination, the Lord in the beginning laid the foundations of the earth and the heavens which are the works of His hands but they all will perish whiles the Lord remains, as in changing a garment He would change them, and as a garments wear out, He would wear them out, rolling them up like a robe. The unchanging Lord who created the earth and the heavens has a plan for this present world, this heavens and earth will perish regardless of how well we preserve it, how great we build edifices on it, they won't last forever, heaven and earth would be replaced completely with a new heaven and a new earth.

The Principles:

- *The seal of the Old Testament is physical circumcision.*
- *The seal of the New Testament is the heart circumcision by the Spirit.*
- *The cross of Christ was and is the altar of God to effect, and enforce the new covenant.*

Now: By the reason of Christ Jesus' work on the cross and His reign on the throne, there are certain assurances for every human who accepts and believes in His name, I would like to call these assurances *"now"*. These assurances do not just have a future reality but also a present everyday reality, their power can be experience now!

Now we stand in Grace;

Our position and place of standing now in Christ is in His Grace. *"We have been justified through faith, we have peace with God through our Lord Jesus Christ, through whom we have gained access by faith into this grace in which we now stand. And we boast in the hope of the glory of God." [Romans 5:1-2 NIV]* We cannot stand anywhere else, no other position or place can be good for us except the grace of our Lord Jesus Christ, if we try to take any other position or place it would be to our own demise.

Now we are justified and have received reconciliation;

Our identity now is that, it is just-as-if we have not sinned. *"We have now been justified by his blood, how much more shall we be saved from God's wrath through him! For if, while we were God's enemies, we were reconciled to him through the death of his Son, how much more, having been reconciled, shall we be saved through his life! Not only is this so, but we also boast in God through our Lord Jesus Christ, through whom we have now received reconciliation. [Romans 5:9-11 NIV]* We now have identical nature as the Lord Jesus Christ, as He is, so are we, there is a *"sameness"* between Christ and those who belong to Christ through the justification by His blood which has brought us reconciliation.

Now we have resurrection;

Our resurrection is a future event and that is true yet it is also a now reality, it is a certain assurance for all who belong to Christ since they died with Christ now. *"Now if we died with Christ, we believe that we will also live with him. For we know that since Christ was raised from the dead, he cannot die again; death no longer has mastery over him. The death he died, he died to sin once for all; but the life he lives, he lives to God." [Romans 6:8-10 NIV]* He, Christ has been raised from the dead never to die again for death does not have mastery over Him and sin as well, but He lives *to* God for evermore, so also it is with all who belong to Christ.

Now we have allegiance to righteousness;

Our allegiance is to righteousness nothing more, nothing less. One cannot belong to Christ and continue to hold allegiance to sin. *"Thanks be to God that, though you used to be slaves to sin, you have come to obey from your heart the pattern of teaching that has now claimed your allegiance. You have been set free from sin and have become slaves to righteousness." [Romans 6:17-19 NIV]* all who are in Christ have being set from slavery of sin into the slavery of righteousness now! And any pattern of teaching that does not claim allegiance to righteousness is in error of Christ. Righteousness is your allied in Christ not sin.

Now we are released from the law;

Our present bond is to Christ and not to the law, for through the body of Christ all who are in Christ have died to the law, we do not belong to the law any longer but we belong to Christ; *"now, by dying to what once bound us, we have been released from the law so that we serve in the new way of the Spirit, and not in the old way of the written code."[Romans 7:6 NIV]* Just as Christ was raised from the dead to sin, all in Christ have now been raised from the dead in sin in order to bear fruit for God. We no longer live in the realm of the flesh so that the sinful passions aroused by the law would be at work in us, that we might bear fruit for death but by bearing fruit to God we serve Him in the new way of the Spirit not the old way of the written code.

Now there is no condemnation;

Our no condemnation from the Father is in Christ now; *"there is now no condemnation for those who are in Christ Jesus, because through Christ Jesus the law of the Spirit who gives life has set you free from the law of sin and death." [Romans 8:1 NIV]*

Now we are God's children and co-heirs with Christ;

Our heirship with Christ is now, we inherit what is *of* Christ *in* Christ and *with* Christ; *"Now if we are children, then we are heirs —heirs of God and co-heirs with Christ, if indeed we share in his sufferings in order that we may also share in his glory." [Romans 8:16 NIV]*

The Cup of Salvation.

If one is to take the salvation that is offered in Christ Jesus and drink of its content, what would one be drinking of? Anyone who lifts the cup of salvation will be drinking from it;

- *Atonement from the sacrifice of Christ Jesus. One becomes at – one with Christ.*
- *Sanctification from the purifying blood of Christ, by the blood a person becomes cleaned and set apart for the use of the Lord.*
- *Justification from the Lord Jesus Christ, a person exchanges and receives the righteousness of Christ. Christ impacts, imparts, imprints and imputes His righteousness on a soul.*
- *Adoption from Christ Jesus into the family of the living God. He gives the legal right and grants the moral authority to be a son of God.*
- *Glorification of the Spirit of glory. The Spirit transforms life from glory to glory into the image of the new son.*

From this cup comes;

- Redemption from sin, death and wrath, regeneration into a new creature, reformation in a new form, renewal into a new soul and rebirth in a new life.
- Restoration into intimacy with the Spirit, inheritance in the fathers' heritage, identity in the Son's nature, insurance into eternal life, and invitation to the royal kingdom.
- Reconciliation to proper position with God, return to a place in the house of God, receiving of the promises of the Lord, revival of power of life, recompense of lost provision, protection, participation, preeminence, parentage, prosperity. Relationship: repent, return, reign. Resurrection: revival, rejoicing, reward, receive.

The Principle-

- *Jesus redeems to reconcile, to renew, to resurrect, to restore, to receive.*
- *Jesus Christ has the Cleansing power, the Healing power, the Resurrection power, the Impartation power, the Saving power, and the Transforming power.*

David and the New Covenant.

David the poetic prophetic psalmist wrote a psalter after he prayed to the LORD when the prophet Nathan came to him, after he had gone in to Bathsheba. It was a prayer for cleansing, purification and pardon. The power of the prayer was only fulfilled in the new covenant through Jesus Christ.

"Have mercy, God, according to your gracious love, according to your unlimited compassion, erase my transgressions. Wash me from my iniquity, cleanse me from my sin. For I acknowledge my transgression; my sin remains continually before me. Against you, you only, have I sinned, and done what was evil in your sight.

As a result, you are just in your pronouncement and clear in your judgment. Indeed, in iniquity I was brought forth; in sin my mother conceived me. Indeed, you are pleased with truth in the inner person, and you will teach me wisdom in my innermost parts. Purge me with hyssop, and I will be clean. Wash me, and I will be whiter than snow. Let me know joy and gladness; let the bones that you have broken rejoice. Hide your countenance from my sins and erase the record of my iniquities. God, create a pure heart in me, and renew a right attitude within me. Do not cast me from your presence; do not take your Holy Spirit from me. Restore to me the joy of your salvation, and let a willing attitude control me. Then I will teach transgressors about your ways, and sinners will turn to you.

Deliver me from the guilt of shedding blood, God, God of my salvation. Then my tongue will sing about your righteousness.

Lord, open my lips, and my mouth will declare your praise. Indeed, you do not delight in sacrifices, or I would give them, nor do you desire burnt offerings. True sacrifice to God is a broken spirit. A broken and chastened heart, God, you will not despise. Show favor to Zion in your good pleasure; and rebuild the walls of Jerusalem. Then you will be pleased with right sacrifices, with burnt offerings, and with whole burnt offerings. Then they will offer bulls on your altar." [Psalm 51:1-19 ISV]

In this Psalter, the Holy Spirit inspired David to pen the pathway to reconciliation and restoration to fellowship through the redemption that the Son Jesus Christ offers. The first phase [of the psalm] deals with the response to the result of sin in man and the second phase deals with the results to the response of dealing with sin in man. Finished work on the cross under the new covenant: Petition Request of David to God about sin and the effects of it, this petition is fulfilled for every human in Christ by the work of the cross of Christ, David asked these things for God to do for him and for that matter deal with the issue of sin for mankind, they are all the work of God by the cross of Christ, not man's work or effort!

10 Provisions of the New Covenant.

- *Pronunciations — pronouncement: sin is a heart issue, it is a heart attitude and action, it is unseen intention that usually ultimately manifest as a seen deed. Sin is both subjective and objective, it has a subject and an object component; if I insult someone, the person becomes the object of my insult yet at the same time the Maker of the person becomes the subject of my insult, if I steal something from someone, the thing stolen and the person becomes the object of my sin yet the primary subject of my sin is the Lord of the person and thing. "Against you, you only, have I sinned, and done what was evil in your sight. As a result, you are just in your pronouncement and clear in your judgment. Indeed, in iniquity I was brought forth — surely, I was sinful at birth —; in sin my mother conceived me — sinful from the time my mother conceived me. Indeed, you are pleased with truth in the inner person — you desired faithfulness even in the womb; and you will teach me wisdom in my innermost parts [that secret place]." [Psalm 51:4-5 NIV] The first truth of life on earth and in the world is the law of sin and death. Humans sin because we are sinful by nature, sinful by the law of birth since we all inherit the nature of our ancestry; you are a sinner not because you sin but you sin because you are a sinner. The first truth of [God about] life is truth. Truth is the first principle of life, without truth everything else becomes a bondage and an ending search for nothingness. The just pronouncement of God against all of humanity due to sin was made against Christ on the cross, God gave His right, righteous verdict for the sinner on the cross and He made a clear judgment that brought finality to sin and its consequences. He became the justified judge, the one who judges and justifies the judged, The Father is pleased with the Son and hence pleased with everyone who believes in the Son.*

- *Pardon of guilt — guiltlessness – peace with God:*
No condemnation: erased transgressions, erased record of iniquities. countenance hidden from sins. deliverance from the guilt of shedding blood. Under the new covenant, the mercy, unfailing gracious love, unlimited great compassion and forgiveness of the Lord is made available to all of humanity. We can gain peace with God through the new covenant in Christ. The greatest pursuit of the human heart is peace, with peace comes wholeness of being and wellness of being. Mankind seeks for peace in all our dealings, for where there is no peace nothing moves on or develops. Through Christ, the shalom and or Hosanna of God comes to all men. Experience the mercy of the Lord according to His gracious unfailing love, according to unlimited great compassion in Christ Jesus. [Psalm 51:1 NIV]

- *Purged, washed, and cleansed as whiter than snow: it is only by the power of the blood of Christ shared on the cross is atonement for sin, sanctification for the Lord and justification before the Lord possible. There is no cleansing and washing from sin through any other means apart from faith in the blood of Jesus Christ. Jesus' blood has the power to purge all of humanity of sin and the power of it, through faith in the blood, we have uncommon standing with the God of gods, and the blood makes everyone who believes in Christ Jesus right with the Father. If the snow is white, then, the blood of Christ cleanses the sinner of his sin whiter than the snow, the blood flowing from the cross purges the sinful man of her sin like the hyssop heals of infections, and it washes from all iniquity. [Psalm 51:7 NIV]*

- *Pure, new, clean, created heart, right attitude and steadfast spirit:*
The heart of the problem of man and for that matter the world is the heart of man. All of humanity is suffering from heart diseases, everything that we see happening around us either good or evil is the baby of the heart. The heart is at the heart of it all. When we see evil, it comes from an evil heart, when we experience wrong it comes from a wrong heart. Only a right heart

or spirit can know right, do right and be right. Right attitudes from the right heart, steadfastness comes from the steadfast spirit and that is what the new covenant in Christ produces, by the power in the new creation in Christ, a new pure and clean heart is created that can now produce rights and rightness. A right spirit is renewed. [Psalm 51:10 NIV]

- *Personal inner truth, faithfulness and wisdom: In the heart of man, the Almighty desires truth, faithfulness and wisdom in the innermost parts. He is pleased with such in the secret place of man's heart and this is what He has accomplished through the power of the new covenant. The new created heart can once again show forth the truth, faithfulness and wisdom of God from the depths of the heart. [Psalm 51:10 NIV]*

- *Presence of the Holy Spirit: The Holy Spirit is not a forceful Spirit, He is the willing Spirit, the free spirit — generous Spirit. He is the Spirit of our adoption into the household of the living God, He is the Spirit of glorification, and He glorifies sons. By the finished work of Christ on the cross, any man who believes in Christ receives the Spirit of glory and will not be cast away from His presence; the Holy Spirit is not taken away from the man in Christ but rather given to be received. He is the willing, free, generous, spirit that enables the man with Christ the free, generous, willing attitude to control, sustain and support the life of the Son of God. [Psalm 51:11-12 NIV]*

- *Praises and the joy of salvation: The Spirit restore the joy of salvation, He reveals the knowledge of joy and gladness, bringing joy to the bones that were broken — crushed, He opens lips and mouth to declare willing praises and tongue to sing about the righteousness in the Lord Jesus Christ. [Psalm 51:12 NIV]*

- *Pleased with and pleasure in the true sacrifice of God: The true sacrifice to God is a broken spirit — a broken [contrite] and chastened heart is the delight of the Lord. The heart willing to offer an acceptable sacrifice of obedience to the Lord, a heart and spirit ready to be submitted to the will of God. [Psalm 51:17 NIV]*

- *Prosperity in Zion — Jerusalem: It is the good pleasure of the Lord to show favor to Zion and rebuild the walls of Jerusalem. The walls of protections, provision, prosperity, progress, peace are all rebuilt to the glory of the Lord. [Psalm 51:18 NIV]*

- *Proclaiming of God's ways: proclaim the ways of the Lord to others, the Lord's ways of salvation so that they will come to the Lord. [Psalm 51:13 NIV]*

A Word to the World of Humanity: *The Recall, Repair, and Return Process of Man.*

God would be justified in making His guilty pronouncement on any man, when He speaks condemnation in His judgment as the judge, He would be clear and blameless, a righteous judge because man indeed sinned against Him and did evil in His sight. But that verdict was passed onto His Son Jesus. Whom He forsook on the cross, on the cross all of man's sin and guilt was on

Jesus thus making Him cry *"my God my God why have you forsaken me?" [Matthew 27:46 NIV]* He completed the work of atoning for the penalty of sin when He said *"it's finished"*, *[John 28:30 NIV]* therefore the debt of sin was cancelled, the distance of separation of sin was covered and there is no more a record of sin. So, the father is no longer counting humanity's sin against us, the Father is recalling all of humanity to return to Him through the Son's repairing process by the Spirit. It is therefore needed and necessary that every man must come back home.

The Loving Father, Abba: *God is Father, a father of the fatherless. He expresses His love towards man. "The Lord is compassionate and gracious, patient, and abundantly rich in gracious love. He does not chasten continuously or remain distant for all time. He neither deals with us according to our sins, nor repays us equivalent to our iniquity. As high as heaven rises above earth, so His gracious love strengthens those who fear Him. As distant as the east is from the west, that is how far He has removed our sins from us. As a father has compassion for his children, so the Lord has compassion for those who fear him. For He knows how we were formed, aware that we were made from dust. The Lord's gracious love remains throughout eternity for those who fear him and his righteous acts extend to their children's children, to those who keep his covenant and to those who remember to observe his precepts." [Psalm 103: 8-10, 11-14, 17-19 ISV]*

Compassion:

God is the father, the Heavenly Father, the only father of fathers. He is full of compassion and grace, patience and love in abundance. From eternity to eternity and throughout all generations, His gracious love remains for all those who fear Him as He extends His righteous acts to the children's children of His godly ones, to all those who keep His covenant and remember to observe His precepts. *[Psalm 103:8, 17-18 ISV]*

Conscious:

He is conscious of His children, He knows how we were formed, aware that we were made from dust. He has deep intimate knowledge of who we are, of our thoughts, desires, actions and ways. He understands us fully. *[Psalm 103:14 ISV]*

Chasten:

This father does not chasten us continually even though He disciplines His children that He loves, so that through discipline His children will produce fruits of righteousness in their lives. He is no an over bearing burdening Father, always looking for our faults and mistakes to punish us. *[Psalm 103:10 ISV]*

Gideon Agyemang

Compensate:

He does not repay His children according to our sin nor in equivalent to our iniquity because He has removed our sins from us just as distant as the east is from the west, and has made His gracious love to strengthen us just as the heaven rises high above the earth. *[Psalm 103:10-12 ISV]*

Cut off:

He does not *take away* His Spirit of Grace from us, neither does He remain distant at all times from us but He is near to convict, comfort, counsel, help, advise, advocate, train and teach us to live well and right before Him. *[Psalm 51:11 ISV]*

Covenant:

He has established His love covenant with us and He is faithful to keep it till the end. An unfailing, unlimited, unending and unequalled covenant with His children. *[Psalm 89:28 ISV]*

Commandment:

He only requires us to keep His covenant and observe His precepts. To live in obedience to Him by His Spirit and to serve Him with reverence. *[Psalm 108:18 ISV]*

Compassion:

God out of His abundant unlimited mercy, unfailing love and gracious kindness deals with us and our sin. He has given us the free offering of His love and sacrifice to save our life. *[Psalm 51:1 ISV]*

Confession:

Humanity no matter who, has sinned against God alone and Him only. This sin is from our conception, and from our inequities and transgression of which we all must acknowledge, even though He knows already. *[Psalm 51:5 ISV]*

Cleanse:

God by His love offering that atones for all sin has erased and blotted out every sin and its effect against all humanity, by the blood of the lamb of God He has washed, purged and purified all humanity from sin and has made us clean and white as snow, His face is no longer upon our sin but the righteousness of His son, because the record of sin has been cancelled, covered and cleansed. *[Psalm 51:7, 9, 103:11-12 ISV]*

Creation:

God desires and is pleased with wisdom and truth in the inner, inward hidden parts of the man so He creates a new heart, a pure and clean heart that he can instill, inspire and in store His truth and wisdom on which the old heart cannot do. He renews the right spirit attitude in this new heart for the heart to act right again. *[Psalm 51:6, 10 ISV]*

Communion:

God provides this new creation with His presence and Holy Spirit for there to be common union between God and the new man, so that fellowship with this new man is possible. The Spirit restores the joy of salvation. *[Psalm 51:12 ISV]*

Choice:

Every human must make the most important choice of life, whether to accept God's process for eternal life or not. It's not an option but a necessity for us all to receive restitution, resurrection, restoration and reconciliation from God, which is by God and based only on God.

High as and Far as: *God is the God of depths, He does everything in deep depths. He creates in depth, He searches deep into heart, and He is deep God.*

Rebuke:

The Lord does not always accuse us, find faults and continually look for room of errors. He does not accuse humanity continuously because all of man's accusations were laid on Christ Jesus on the cross. He does not deal with us and treat us according to our sins nor repay us equivalent to our iniquity because of Christ, He is our 'deal' and our 'equivalent' in mercy, and unlimited compassion. *[Psalm 103:9-10 ISV]*

Remain distant:

The Lord does not harbor, hide and keep His anger about our sin forever, He does not maintain a dispute continuously. He does not distant Himself from us but always comes close to us. His presence is always with His son to help us overcome the world and sin. *[Psalm 103:8 ISV]*

Repay:

The Lord does not deal and treat us as our sin deserves. The rewards of our sin are not repaid to us, it has been paid by Jesus, and the Lamb of God who took away the sin of the world hence we cannot be repaid with it. *[Psalm 103:10 ISV]*

Remove:

The Lord has removed our sins from us. By the work of Jesus Christ which He finished on the cross, in the tomb, and on the throne, He the Lord has dealt with our sins by removing it all. The removal length, breath, height and distance is like measuring the east from the west, the heavens above from the depths of the earth below. *[Psalm 103:11-12 ISV]*

Restore:

The Lord has restored unto us what we lost due to sin. The loss of our position, power, place et al. The length and depth of the restoration of God's grace, glory, love, riches... transcends all understanding, it goes beyond all measure as the heavens are high from the earth and the east is from the west. *[Psalm 51:12 ISV]*

The Blessed One: Anyone who accepts Christ Jesus is the blessed one, why? Because through the eternal purpose accomplished in Christ, that man has access to these; "Blessed is the one whose transgressions are forgiven; whose sins are covered. Blessed is the one whose sin the Lord does not count against them and in whose spirit is no deceit. When I kept silent, my bones wasted away through my groaning all day long. For day and night your hand was heavy on me; my strength was sapped as in the heat of summer. Then I acknowledged my sin to you and did not cover up my iniquity. I said, "I will confess my transgressions to the Lord." And you forgave the guilt of my sin". [Psalm 32:1-5 NIV]

Cancelled:

Like owing a debt with a bank and having no means to pay, being in danger of facing the penalty for defaulting on the debt and someone else comes to pay it fully- the person "covers" the debt, without a need to pay back to the person. That is what Jesus has done for us with our sins, He covered the debt and penalty of sin. No man owes the debt and penalty anymore, Man you are covered! And made the righteousness of God. Jesus Christ has imputed and imparted His righteousness on us. *[Psalm 32:1-2 NIV]*

Covered:

Sin created a vast separation between man and his maker that no one could cover. The separation distance that sin brought, that distance which no man could overcome, Jesus covered it all. The distance of heaven to earth, earth to the depths of the earth and back to earth and heaven again, He covered it when He came down from heaven to earth by the virgin birth, when He went from earth to the depth of the earth and rose again to the highest. *[Psalm 32:1-2 NIV]*

Count Against:

God is not counting sin against anybody even the world, in God's book of accounting, He has reconciled with our debt of sin and (re)consolidated it through the obedience of Jesus. He says you have no Charge of sin in the Court of righteousness and Justice. Any crime committed in the book of God is judged and acquitted. - Imparted Righteousness. *[Psalm 32:1-2 NIV]*

Conceit-Deceit:

No one must be conceited and deceitful with and about sin in his spirit. We must all be sincere with our sin before God, open and unashamed or afraid but in submission to His mercy and grace in Christ Jesus. *[Psalm 32:5 NIV]*

Cover up:

One must acknowledge, accept and agree with the force of sin, not "cover up" and rather confess to the Lord, and renounce it in order to accept God's forgiveness and the power to live righteously. *[Psalm 32:5 NIV]*

Guilt of sin:

Sin has weight, it generates guilt of conscience, and it saps the joy of life and produces sorrow of the spirit and soul when one keeps silent about it. But the power of the Spirit and the blood of Jesus cleanse all dead works and weight of the guilt of sin on the conscience. The blessed one is the forgiven, the covered. *[Psalm 32:5 NIV]*

Remain Standing: *"Lord, if you were to record iniquities, Lord, who could remain standing? But with you there is forgiveness, so that we can, with reverence, serve you. For with the Lord there is gracious unfailing love, mercy is found with Him along with abundant full great redemption. And He Himself will redeem Israel from all its sins." [Psalm 130:3-4, 7-8 ISV]*

Record:

It's amazing the God who sees all things, hears all things and knows all things and yet doesn't keep track of sins, He does not have record of our sin, and He is not in the business of recording sin, why because if He was to do that no one can stand. No one could be without sin and be in right standing with Him since all man have sinned and fallen short of His glory, and sin has become a human nature. But there is hope. *[Psalm 130:3 ISV]*

Redeemer:

He Himself is the redeemer, He redeems the man bound to sin's yoke and chains. He does not only record sins because no one could stand but because He Himself is the redeemer who redeems all from sin. From His unfailing gracious love and mercy, He provides the great abundant and full redemption of man. He alone could redeem man and so He did it. *[Psalm 130:7-8 ISV]*

Redeemed:

The redeemed of the Lord must declare and tell their story, as a testimony to all. For she has been forgiven of all sin and must therefore serve the Lord with reverence. *[Psalm 130:4 ISV]*

Reverence:

Let all of mankind revere the Lord, let us serve Him with fear and trembling due to the awesomeness and gracious of His love towards us. *[Psalm 130:4 ISV]*

The Blessing Soul: *"Bless the Lord, my soul, and all that is within me, bless his holy name. Bless the Lord, my soul, and never forget any of his benefits: He continues to forgive all your sins, he continues to heal all your diseases, he continues to redeem your life from the pit, and he continually surrounds you with gracious love and compassion. He keeps satisfying you with good things, and he keeps renewing your youth like the eagle's. The Lord continually does what is right, executing justice for all who are being oppressed." [Psalm 103:1-5 ISV]*

Bear in mind Considerably:

Always bear in mind of the Lord's benefits, never forget any of them, for the Lord is good and His mercies, love, grace endures forever. *[Psalm 103:1-2 ISV]*

Benefits Continually:

He always keeps giving and satisfying us with benefits, the benefits of; forgiveness of all sins, healing of all diseases, redeeming of life from the pit, surrounding with gracious love and compassion, satisfying with good things, renewing youth like the eagle's, doing what is right, and executing justice for all who are being oppressed. *[Psalm 103:2-5 ISV]*

Blessings Conferred on His Name:

Bless the name of the Lord, confer on Him the blessing of the hearts, the fruits of our lips. Praise Him, Honor Him, Magnify Him and Glorify Him. *[Psalm 103:1 ISV]*

One the basis of these, therefore, everyone is;

- *To Realize, be aware and acknowledge our sin, accept, believe and acknowledge the Lordship of Jesus Christ and His salvation by the cross.*
- *To Repent, be ready for actions and attitudes to change. To change the minds and heart to come to the Lord.*
- *To Return, accept and arrive back to fellowship by the finished work of Christ on the cross. Come back to the father through the way of truth and life of the Son.*
- *To be Reborn by the Spirit, regenerated by the Spirit of the Son to reflect His image and glory.*
- *To Renew, to be awaken again by the Spirit. Revived, resurrected in spirit, soul and body.*
- *To be Restored as sons and heirs of the father.*
- *To Rejoice, appreciate the Savior and salvation. Rejoice because you have been made right again and glorified.*

My Humble Request To You.

Turn to God in Jesus' name, Talk to God in Jesus' name and Trust in God in Jesus' name.
Believe in Jesus Christ as Lord and receive the Spirit of Christ.
Confess and profess the truths and wisdom of the principles of the message of the gospel of Christ and live in its reality.

Printed in the United States
By Bookmasters